WISHING YOU THE BEST OF HEALTH

D0768043

Candles Burned in Chicago

A History of 53 Memorial

Commemorations of the Warsaw

Ghetto Uprising

by

The Midwest Jewish Council

authorHOUSE™

1663 LIBERTY DRIVE, SUITE 200
BLOOMINGTON, INDIANA 47403
(800) 839-8640
WWW.AUTHORHOUSE.COM

© 2004 The Midwest Jewish Council
All Rights Reserved.

No part of this book may be reproduced, stored in a retrieval system, or transmitted by any means without the written permission of the author.

First published by AuthorHouse 07/27/04

ISBN: 1-4184-8633-7 (e)
ISBN: 1-4184-8632-9 (sc)

Library of Congress Control Number: 2004095380

Printed in the United States of America
Bloomington, Indiana

This book is printed on acid-free paper.

The Midwest Jewish Council

Editor
Kenan Heise

Contributing editors:
N. Sue Weiler
Lianne C. Casten

The cover photo was taken April 9,1961 at the 18th Commemoration,Those in the picture include, Johanna Brainin (second from left) who at 18 months was smuggled out of the Warsaw Ghetto in a coffin, Cipora Fox Katz (second from right) who was found in a cave by U.S. troops during the liberation, Herman Bush (left) president of the Midwest Jewish Council, Ann Hirsch (center) Ben Aronin (right) author of the book, "Eichman's Accomplices," who wrote a dramatic portrayal presented at the meeting

About the Editor

Kenan Heise who edited this book, is a retired journalist, a prolific author and a person deeply committed to human and civil rights. Whenever he wrote an obituary for the Chicago Tribune about a Holocaust survivor, he deliberately included the names of any of their immediate family members who had perished in the Shoah, making it their obituaries also.

N. Sue Weiler contributed the preliminary research on this book.

Milton Herst, President
Midwest Jewish Council

*Dedicated to the Heroes and Martyrs
of the Warsaw Ghetto*

Foreword

By Leon M. Despres

This book tells the amazing story of 54 years of effort by a group of Jewish Chicagoans to commemorate the murder of 350,000 Jews in the Warsaw Ghetto.

In 1944, when these Chicagoans learned of the murder and of the heroic resistance by the last Warsaw Ghetto residents, they determined that the events must be made known to all America so that they might never be forgotten. Except for the fact of past emigration from Europe, these Chicagoans would have been part of the resistance bands. But for their presence in America, they would have lost their lives in the Warsaw slaughter. They determined that they must do all within their power to mobilize the world to prevent a recurrence. So, for 54 years, they undertook to publicize the Warsaw events dramatically and to point out to society the lesson of the events, namely, that humanity must work unceasingly for a just world in which evil cannot triumph as it did.

From 1944 to 1996, this group of Jewish Chicagoans and their friends mounted stirring national meetings, candlelight commemoration dramatic presentations, and gifted discussions so that the heroism of the Warsaw Ghetto fighters and the tragedy of the victims might never be forgotten.

This book tells the story of the annual meetings and their organization. The reader can only be deeply impressed that the thrust of these was not merely to rehearse the past lest it be forgotten, but also to look to the future. For 54 years, speakers at the commemorations stressed the need for present and future action to build a society in which a Warsaw Ghetto slaughter could not take place. The major commemorations, year after year required cooperation and organization, which were not always easy to achieve. Since the effort was open to everyone to support and participate, it attracted also its share of radicals and dissenters. If such individuals were also among the residents of the Warsaw Ghetto, why not in Chicago? Creative differences of opinion had to be ironed out with tact and firmness. They attracted the attention of the Chicago Police

Department espionage unit, which described some of the participants as Communist Party sympathizers or members.

The Jewish Chicagoans who carried forward the commemoration effort had, in themselves, all the elements of heroism and tragedy of the Warsaw Ghetto. So, year after year, they resolutely continued their effort and achieved effectiveness and prestige for what they were doing.

In part their effort was sustained by a pride in the bravery and resistance of the last units in the Ghetto.

The reader of this book will note the continuing emphasis on youth. It was not enough that contemporaries of the Warsaw fighters remember what happened. They believed it was essential that their new generation know what occurred and forestall repetition.

At the end of the 54 years, the story became well known. Although it is still necessary to retell the story, remind the world what happened, and impress the need to prevent a repetition, a specific commemoration meeting in Chicago is no longer necessary. The lesson has been well learned and widely disseminated, thanks to the Midwest Jewish Council and other like-minded Americans. What one significant group did single-handedly is the story of this book.

Reflections

"We rededicate ourselves to holding to the cause of preventing a repetition of the tragedy of the Warsaw Ghetto."

Jack Fishbein, editor and publisher of the *Chicago Jewish Sentinel* at the 2nd Commemoration 1945

"Then I came to Chicago and I wanted to talk about the war. And the people would say, 'I didn't know about it.' I'd speak at temples and ask them, 'What do you mean, you didn't know? Didn't you write your relatives in Europe? Did you get answers?' And all I heard was, 'We didn't know.' Like some kind of hypnotic phrase over and over. And I'd remind them, 'You really didn't know about the Warsaw Ghetto and how it was burning? Why didn't you know? The government knew; the State Department knew. The stories of the Ghetto Uprising began to appear in the papers, in the newsreels. And you didn't know?'"

Barbara Steiner, Warsaw Ghetto Uprising survivor

***

"For years we have been calling the attention of humanity in general, and our people in particular, to the most dreadful catastrophe that befell the world in general and the Jewish people in particular, during the loathsome savage Nazi regime. We have attempted to keep, by these memorial meetings, the memory of this cycloramic catastrophe alive not only for the purpose of lamenting our particular losses as Jews, but also to waken humanity to the possibility of its recurrence, if tyranny is encouraged to flourish and the germs of hate and bigotry are allowed to spread.

"I don't know to what extent we have succeeded in keeping the memory of this catastrophe alive or have alerted humanity to the lurking dangers of forgetfulness and its subsequent indifference. We realize that humanity is bent on forgetting, being that forgetfulness is one of the greatest frailties of the human race. I hope though that with our memorial meetings and other similarly arranged

we have succeeded at least in preventing humanity from total forgetfulness."

From a 1959 letter by Rabbi Abraham Abramowitz to the 16th annual commemoration from Israel. He was co-founder of the commemorations in Chicago of the Warsaw Ghetto Uprising.

Introduction

An Annual Candle Lighting Ceremony in Chicago

Our feelings are deep, our commitments are equally deep. We must never let any injustice to any people go by without commitment to that struggle. We light candles for a vision for the hope of the future. These are candles against the darkness
Heather Booth, speaking at the 45th Commemoration of the Warsaw Ghetto Uprising

***

Each spring, from 1944 through 1996, Chicago witnessed a commemoration, with deep and trenchant meaning. Accompanied by words (in Hebrew, Yiddish and English), speeches, songs, performances and ceremonies, it commemorated the heroism and tragedy of Jewish men, women, and children involved in the Warsaw Ghetto Uprising.

The ceremonial lighting of candles memorialized them and eventually developed into a ritual passing on to the next generation of the responsibility lest it happen again for remembering, for not forgetting who the martyrs and heroes were and for holding in esteem what they had done.

A 1952 *Sentinel* article described the Chicago Jews who instituted this remembrance in 1944 as a group:

Stubbornly devoted to the principles for which the Warsaw Ghetto fighters fought and bled...they form(ed) a permanent committee at perpetuating the memory of those who died for *Kiddush Hashem.* (Santification of the name)

***

The organized effort was initiated by the Chicago chapter of the American Federation of Polish Jews (AFPJ) led by Herman Bush, Rabbi Abraham Abramowitz and a number of volunteers.

In a copyrighted piece in the Fall, 1999 issue of *Western States Jewish History*, N. Sue Weiler described who else were part of the initial effort:

The earliest participants were primarily immigrants from Poland who had escaped the Holocaust, but identified with their families who died and suffered. "They were joined," she continued, "by survivors sharing their horrible experiences and educators teaching children about the evils."

The leaders determined from the beginning that these programs were to include speakers who would talk about current issues such as anti-Semitism, the State of Israel, racism and social injustice. They sought to involve not only Jews, but also representatives of people from all walks of life who saw the connection to issues affecting the larger community.

As the war came to an end, those organizing and promoting the commemoration also became involved in relief efforts to send food, clothing and medication to help keep alive the Jews in Europe who had survived the Holocaust.

In the 1950s, the group sponsoring the annual commemotation formally reorganized and became the Midwest Jewish Council (MJC.)

Chapter 1

Barbara Steiner:
A Warsaw Ghetto Survivor
with a Message for Chicago

Mrs. Steiner, a resident of Skokie, was active over the years in various capacities in helping put on the Chicago Warsaw Ghetto Uprising Commemorations. She came to the U.S. in the early 1950s. Along with her husband, Arnold, and their son, she temporarily at first lived with an aunt in New York. She was very much in need of someone with whom to talk about her experiences.

Her aunt told her, "Barbara, forget the past. You now live in America; this is a new life. Drop the past. You really don't want to know how your own mother died, or your brothers. This is gone. Stop it."

The following excerpts are from the transcript of an interview with Mrs Steinerr in her Skokie home.

Then I came to Chicago and I wanted to talk about the war. And the people would say, "I didn't know about it." I'd speak at temples and ask them, "What do you mean, you didn't know? Didn't you write your relatives in Europe? Did you get answers?" And all I heard was, "We didn't know." Like some kind of hypnotic phrase over and over. And I'd remind them, "You really didn't know about the Warsaw Ghetto and how it was burning? Why didn't you know? The government knew; the U.S. State Department knew. The stories of the Ghetto uprising began to appear in the papers, in the newsreels. And you didn't know?"

And then I began to ask myself, "Why?" And I had to answer—however painful. Jews are a cheap commodity—even to themselves. My fellow Jews had a deep need to deny all this horror—both in Europe and in the U.S. There was too much fear, and if they accepted reality, there would be too many

1

mandates to act. And they were not prepared to act. They needed to be comfortable. And if Europeans— the survivors come to America, with their accents and their customs and their memories, they might take away all that the U.S. Jews have already achieved.

They might bring out that anti-Semitism which Jews always feared. But, there was in addition some jealousy, a sense of competition, perhaps some guilt—who knows.

***

(The following excerpts come after a tender recounting of her early life in a wealthy, caring home in a gentile section of Warsaw followed by an increasing persecution of her family and other Jews by the Polish authorities and then, the invading German army.)

The worst began with 1941. I was 15. It was so cold. My father was getting sicker, minute by minute. One day I got home and he couldn't walk anymore. He was in bed. He couldn't even make some tea. He told me, "Take books and burn them. Instead of them burning the books, you do it."

I must have fallen asleep. I woke up and he couldn't speak anymore. My dad was in a coma. He was dying. I ran to the doctor. "Help me. My father is dying. I give you the coat I am wearing." I'm running with a stick, tearing off my clothes. The doctor answered. "What do you want from the man? He's dying."

I ran back to Papa. I took him in my arms. I started to cry. He died with me holding him. It was the most tragic moment of my life. I had no money for a funeral. They promised they'd bury my father, but they put him on a wagon with all the other dead bodies and put him in a common grave.

He was only in his 40s. I remember his words: "Everyone can take away from you all of your possessions. They have to kill you to take away your knowledge." He knew: Polish, German, Hebrew, Yiddish, French and was studying English.

***

Meanwhile, here is my brother and mother and I am afraid for them. I ran out. I was so afraid of them. They were both dying. I thought it was catching. There was a little store across the street. It sold food on the food stamps. The owner, who had a little girl, asked, "Would you want to watch my baby?"

"Sure," I said. She kept me in the cold store and gave me very little for my work. I covered myself with paper. One day my mother came. She knew I was there. She said she was going to her sister. She asked me to walk with her. "I can't, Mom. Not now."

Two hours later, my cousin came to tell me my mother died. How could I have not gone with her? May God forgive me.

My brother was in the little room when I came back. The woman where I worked gave me a little sandwich to take to her child. My brother asked me to give him the bread. I didn't. The bread was not mine to give. He was so good, so patient. But the bread belonged to the child. How could I have done this? I betrayed my own brother. I will live with this the rest of my life. As to my other brother, we never heard from them or their baby.

***

Fall, 1942 saw the largest deportation out of the Ghetto. The Uprising began April 19, 1943. By that time the vast majority of the Ghetto's 500,000 Jews were dead and or had been exported to death camps. To describe the hunger in the city is almost impossible. Hunger hurts. The children from Bosnia and Somalia look just like those in the Ghetto.

I walked in the Ghetto. I too was very hungry. The Ghetto was nearly empty. I was crying. I was 16. How did I walk over the bodies in the Ghetto? If you take away a person's dignity, if you de-humanize him, make him hungry like an animal, that same person who was wonderful becomes half an animal.

I met someone my age who told me about a family—a couple looking for someone to watch their children. They had a grocery store and sold food from food stamps. They had a little child. Wouldn't it be wonderful! I flew to their apartment.

"I'm sorry," she said, looking at me with disgust. "I cannot let you in." True, I was filthy. I had walked aimlessly through empty buildings and hadn't washed myself in days.

I was just about to leave the apartment—a completely strange building and suddenly the Germans were surrounding the block. I had no idea where to hide. I ran down the steps. A little window opening and I jumped into the basement. The German saw me; yet the basement was full of feathers. I sank into them and disappeared. After an hour or two, after the shooting and my own crying stopped, I emerged. I met a little girl who also hid. We were the only two in the whole long block. I went upstairs to the same apartment with my new friend, and the door was wide open. Everything was there as the housewife had left it.

We found some food and ate quite a bit. We stuffed ourselves. After eating, we realized that we

4

wanted to clean up. The other girl was dirty, but not as filthy as I was. In addition to the dirt, I had feathers all over me.

We used soap that was left behind to clean up. Also, there were clothes, including underwear, and we took them too. I used a scissors to try to cut things so they might fit us.

We went out. There was no more one big ghetto. The Germans made little ghettos, each surrounded with walls. They made little factories—broom, uniform, machinery. We walked to the broom factory. And they took us in and the factory was huge. They gave us a little apartment with six girls living together. We received food from the factory owners. It got a little better. I got to look a little better. Every second day there were selections. I was with the girls from a strange village with many children. It's 1942. I was sitting in a room. The Germans surrounded the building, and there was no place to hide.

My father's voice told me to hide in this special room. I knew it was my Papa, and I would listen.

"Push a china cabinet to cover the door," he said.

On top there was a window on the door. We took some clothes and pillows and covered the window. We spilled water in the other two rooms. Then we left the doors open and made it look as if no one else was in the apartment. All 25 of us—hiding in this little room. There was not even enough time to nail the piece of wood back someone held it with his foot.

The Germans came in. They looked disgusted, hollered how dirty it all was. They hit the china cabinet. Nothing fell down. Then they walked out; they hadn't found us. Twenty-five of us were safe for the moment. I said to the group, 'I see my father.' He told me, "Don't stay here." The factory was a huge building. I heard him say, "Go to the factory." In the

5

middle of the night, I got up and said, "I'm going." My father told me to go. I sneaked back to the factory and the Germans found the others.

Finally, the Uprising started.

Chapter 2

The Warsaw Ghetto Uprising and the Reason to Commemorate It

The special meaning of the Warsaw Ghetto Uprising rests in the fact that the Jews there were the first civilians in all Occupied Europe to dare to carry out a major revolt against the German military. Others—inspired, would follow their example—in different cities and even in death camps such as Treblinka would light the torch they had raised high. And future generations, we now know would memorialize them in the phrase, "Never again."

In the 1963 edition of his book, *Uprising in the Warsaw Ghetto,* Ber Mark begins:

The most heroic act of armed Jewish resistance to Hitler's program of mass murder—the Warsaw Ghetto Uprising—continues to attract the attention not only of Jews but of all peoples of the world. Rarely in the history of mankind has there been such an extraordinary struggle—extraordinary in its circumstances, its superhuman heroism, and its tragic end. The example of the Warsaw Ghetto fighters remains a guiding light for all freedom-loving people; remarkably, as April 19, 1943, draws further away in time, the more inspiring become the images of the Jewish rebels, the more deeply felt is the reverence of the survivors, and the more urgent is the need to learn who these heroic men and women were and what their struggle was like.

While the principal purpose of this book is not a recounting of the noble and heroic fighting in the Warsaw Ghetto, the encouraging of its readers to look back on what happened and to reflect on it, is paramount.

The materials now available did not exist when the first or even the majority of annual commemorations were being held in Chicago. Fortunately, they have been written, published and made available.

These include among others:

Ber Mark's book, listed above (Shocken Books,1963.)

Vladka Meed's *On Both Sides of the Wall: Memoirs from the Warsaw Ghetto,* (Holocaust Library, 1979). She was a Warsaw Ghetto fighter and survivor. Her book tells in minute detail of the fight, the fighters, their sacrifices and their heroism. She also describes how she, because of her Aryan looks, was able to move between the Ghetto and the rest of the city, bringing help, money, arms, food from the outside to the fighters who chose to remain.

A pamphlet (available on the Internet) Marek Edelman's *The Warsaw Ghetto: The 45th Anniversary of the Uprising* (a pamphlet, Interpress Publishers.)

• Finally, the autobiography of Skokie resident, Barbara Steiner, which is excerpted later in this book. Several basic, underlying facts help tell the significance of the Uprising.

***

What preceded the Uprising

Before the war, the city had been the center of Jewish life and culture in Poland. The Warsaw Jewish community, with a population of 350,000, was the largest in Europe and the second largest in the world, behind only New York.

When the Ghetto was changed into a holding-pen prison in October 1940, large numbers of Jews were gathered from throughout the rest of Poland.

Between October 1940 and July 1942, close to 100,000 Warsaw Ghetto Jews died, according to Ber Mark, "of hunger, epidemic, superhuman slave labor in concentration camps, or through mass execution." Then, the mass exterminations began with 300,000 either deported to the death camp at Treblinka or shot on the spot.

In his booklet, Marek Edelman describes the mindset of those who somehow had temporarily managed to survive this:

> The Jews—beaten, stepped upon, slaughtered without the slightest cause—lived in constant fear. There was only one punishment for failure to obey regulations—death—while careful obedience to the rules did not protect against a thousand more and more fantastic degradations, more and more acute persecutions, recurrent acts of terror, more far-reaching regulations. To top it all, the unwritten law of collective responsibility was being applied against the Jews. Thus in the first days of November 1939, 53 male inhabitants of the 9 Nalewski Street apartment house were summarily shot for the beating of a Polish policeman by one of the tenants. This occurrence, the first case of mass punishment, intensified the feeling of panic amongst the Warsaw Jews. Their fear of the Germans now took on unequalled forms.

Despite their decimation and this imminent sense of fear and panic, a group of principally young people created a revolt heard around the world and subsequently memorialized for the ages.

***

How the Uprising came about

The revolt built on an earlier, unsuccessful attempt; and was engineered by two groups of youths that had long disagreed about fundamental goals. The situation, however, was desperate. Writing in the June 2003 issue of *Socialism Today*, John Dale described it:

> Hope of survival had been replaced with the expectation of death: would it be met in Treblinka or fighting in the Ghetto? Despair turned to determination.

He continued:

> There was a long history of rivalry between the Bund, which stood for a socialist Poland with emancipation of Jews as a national minority, the left-wing Zionist movements, which stood for a socialist Jewish state in Palestine. Now the remaining members of these organizations recognized a united front was needed.

> Groups of five or seven from the same organization formed combat units. A joint commander was appointed, Mordechai Anielewicz, a 23-year-old who had been organizing youth groups since before the war.

Their force, the Jewish Fighting Organization, staged an aborted revolt in January 1943 during a round-up by the Nazis. They managed to kill several SS soldiers and free a group of Jews being marched to the train for Treblinka with weapons obtained from the Polish Home Army. The better-planned and more successful action occurred three months later.

***

The experiences of Barbara Steiner

The following personal account of it by Barbara Steiner is from her forthcoming autobiography:

After this *aktion,* it was very quiet for about two months, until the Uprising. The Nazis led us to believe that they were treating us better. They even allowed us to bake *matzos* for the first time in the Ghetto. Of course, all the time they were plotting our annihilation. They were preparing to liquidate the Ghetto--removing everyone and sending them to the death camps. This is the legendary sadism of the Nazis. How can anyone call them human beings?

At this time, a small group of young people began organizing and discussing an uprising. We all swore that if we were caught we would give our lives, but never, never give another person's name to the Nazis. Only a very few people knew where we would build the bunker and so, at the beginning I didn't know where it would be. We talked about getting food and medication for the bunkers. Some of our people were willing to smuggle themselves out of the Ghetto to get ammunition from the Aryan side. We tried to get as much money as possible from wherever we could. This really was the birth of the uprising.

I was trained before the war a little in first aid, so my job, when the Uprising came, would be to minister to the injured. There were ten people in my group. Everyone knew just what his job was and didn't know much about the other people. That was the safest way to do things. We kept the existence of the group secret from all the other people as well.

The Uprising began the first day of Passover, April 19, 1943. Passover is a time of celebration of our freedom from bondage and here we were more enslaved than we had ever been before, our people being decimated and tortured. This date was not a random choice for the Nazis. Hitler's birthday was the 20th of April and as a birthday present, his troops wanted to give him a Warsaw free of all Jews.

Working in the factory, I knew some things, but I also knew people who knew a lot more than I did. They trusted me. Two or three days before the Uprising, I worked with them late at night making Molotov cocktails in the basement of my apartment building. You had to put a piece of material as a wick and the gasoline in each of a large assortment of bottles that had been collected. We left them there on a table covered over by a blanket.

I believe it was the evening of April 18, we heard by word of mouth that the Ghetto had been surrounded by the SS, Latvian and Ukrainian troops as well as tanks. We were told to go down to the bunkers. Each person was assigned a specific bunker. My roommate wasn't part of the uprising movement and was not assigned to this bunker, but when I began going, she followed me. We had to let her in, there was no way we could leave her out. For one thing, we knew she would be exposed and killed or taken immediately and secondly, if she were captured, the Nazis might torture her and find out where we were hidden.

To get to the bunker, we had to go down to a first floor apartment. The windowsill was wider than a normal sill. We lifted the windowsill and inside there was a ladder going down to the basement, which we climbed down. When we reached the basement, there was another ladder, not visible from the top, that led to the bunker which was below the basement level. This bunker was constructed amazingly well. There was so much work and ingenuity in planning this, considering the incredibly limited resources we had.

The bunker had been planned for 30 people, but there were 35 in there now. We had some bunk beds, food, electricity that was connected to the city electricity, a well to provide us with water and a tunnel connected to the sewer system. Fresh air came in through the chimney above. We could have survived for a year in this manner.

When we became involved in the Uprising, all of us made a pact that we would not allow the Nazis to take us. We knew that we had no chance to survive, but we wanted to die with dignity. We wanted history to record that it was not true that Jews went like sheep to the slaughter. We were prepared to fight to the last person.

The first day, the women sat in the bunker and the men were on the rooftops or balconies with homemade Molotov cocktails and the few guns we had, waiting for the Nazis. At first, a German tank tried to enter the broom factory and was promptly blown up by Molotov cocktails. This surprised the Nazis and they turned around and fled. Then we heard them on bullhorns asking us come out of the bunkers. They promised they would resettle us to the small town of Trevniki where we could work and survive the war. The man speaking, Commander Stroop, the officer in charge of the liquidation, gave us his word of honor. Of course, our answer was "Never again will we allow you to take us to kill us. We will fight to the end."

Every day the fighting began when the Nazis started bombing the Ghetto with artillery pieces. The Nazis would never walk into the Ghetto. They shot from outside of the Ghetto with artillery and grenades, but they never actually came into the Ghetto. The reason they didn't was because they were afraid for their lives.

At this point, I would like to mention the brave young boys. They stood on the roofs and balconies of the buildings with Molotov cocktails and a few guns. They knew that there was a good possibility that they would be killed at any moment, but they fought so bravely against the mighty Nazi army. They would shoot any German who entered and they threw these Molotov cocktails over the wall to the German side as well. That's how we were able to kill the enemy.

During the Uprising I found out that there were quite a few bunkers and that the famous one at Mila 18 was very close to ours. This bunker was the headquarters of the Uprising and I later found out that the commander and hero of the entire Uprising was Mordechai Anielewicz, a young man whom I had known in his student days. Our bunker was located at Szwientojerska 30. In fact, we were in communication with them during the Uprising.

Here's how we were able to communicate. The Germans were afraid to enter the Ghetto during the nighttime hours. So at this time, some of the people from the bunker, usually two men, would try to communicate and find out what was going on and how the situation was developing outside our bunker. Inside the bunker, we received instructions through radio or phone system. For example, we would be warned to turn down the lights, to be quiet because the Nazis were close. I even remember one young man, with tears in his voice, told us to pray. A little later we got the news that this young man had been killed.

The atmosphere in the bunker was heavy with sadness. We were frightened, praying for a miracle and feeling so strongly that these were the last minutes of our lives. Every one of us tried to remember our parents, our dreams, our hopes and all that we had before the war. We were certain one person with the power to destroy us would end it all. To think that one individual, who looked like a human being but was, in fact, such a terrible devil, could have this kind of power over the lives and deaths of so many people.

At that moment I questioned G-d. "Where are you, G-d?" "Why do you allow this to happen?" "Haven't we suffered enough already?" "Wasn't it enough to lose all our loved ones?" 'Wasn't it enough to see the hunger, the starvation, the beatings and killings and the streets full of the dead and dying?' "Do we now have to pay with the only thing we have - our lives?" "And why, why G-d?" "WHY?"

Still, after everything I'd been through and seen, I still wanted so desperately to survive.

After two weeks, the Nazis realized that they would not be able to get us out of the bunkers so they began burning each and every building in the Ghetto. The fire was tremendous, it seemed like the whole world was in flames. Because we got our fresh air from the outside, we knew that we could not survive even though we were in the bunker. We knew the building would eventually collapse on us and that the supply of fresh air which came through the chimney, would be overcome by the flames and smoke.

The young man in charge of our bunker told us what to do when the fires began. We were supposed to wait until the building burned to the first floor. We were to wet ourselves, our clothing, our hair and hold a wet piece of cloth to our mouths to help keep the smoke from choking us.

Around May 2nd or 3rd, I'm not certain of the day at this time, but I think it was a few days before I was captured, they began burning all the buildings in the entire broom factory. We waited until the fire reached the first floor, wetted ourselves and, holding cloths to our mouths, all came out of the bunker.

Some people decided, rather than be captured by the Nazis, they would commit suicide and they took a pill rather than leave the bunker. I remember a couple of people tried to escape through the sewer system and they killed everyone down there.

What we saw was an inferno consuming the building. This was a very large apartment building and we were in the courtyard of the building. Much of the building was already destroyed.

How can I describe this terrible tragedy this horrible, unbelievable scene? We knew that we were unable to do anything about this, knowing there is no place to hide, knowing that you have to come out of the bunker or you will be suffocated or burned alive, knowing that nobody was listening to or cared about our cries? We held our cloths to our mouths and tried to hide as best we could. We prayed, we cried, we knew that we needed a miracle to survive.

I saw huge pieces of burning wood falling from the building. One woman had a very young baby, a few months old at most. She was holding him in a small bundle that was the way babies were carried in Europe at this time. There was a pillow and a board of some kind. The baby was laid on the board and covered with a cloth on top that was tied for the baby's protection. As she held the baby, a large fiery piece of wood came flying down off the building and fell into the bundle where the baby was lying. Everyone began screaming and the woman was forced to abandon the bundle. I remember she was half crazy, screaming and crying, knowing that there was nothing she could do to save the baby. It was one of the most horrible things I had to witness. There we were, with no help from people or from G-d.

On May 5th the Nazis found us all. Several of us were trying to hide in a burned-out building. I walked out with the rest of the people. It was a sunny day, the fire was burning around us, the smoke was unbelievable; the screaming; the praying still rings in my ears. But I know that even as we were leaving, the resistance fighting continued.

The Nazis gathered us together, took all the men, supposedly to clean the bunkers. About 10 of us, young girls were marched to a wall that was part of the burned-out building. They told us to face the wall and reach our hands up. I was certain they were going to kill us. I said the Sh'ma *(Hear O Israel: the Lord is our God, the Lord is One!)* and prepared to die. I heard some shooting, but after a few minutes they told us to turn around. They hadn't killed any of us, they were just laughing, showing us that they could have killed us if they had wanted to. For them this was a little amusement.

Were they really human or were they just vicious animals on two legs?

Chapter 3

Chicago: May 1, 1944
The 1ˢᵗ COMMEMORATION

The need to respond to the terrible annihilation of millions of their people and the crushing of the Warsaw Ghetto Uprising led the Chicago branch of the American Federation of Polish Jews (AFPJ) at their annual meeting February 17,1944 to organize a memorial meeting.

These were their fellow Jews living in the country of their ancestors—many of them friends, relatives and former neighbors—who had held up their chains and shaken them for the world to see and to hear.

The purpose of the commemoration, was to eulogize, commemorate and perpetuate the sounds and sights of those who fought and died in the Ghetto. This first gathering was to be a citywide Yahrzeit (memorial), created by people who were determined to keep the memories alive through focusing on the story of those Jews who fought back during World War II in the Warsaw Ghetto as well as in other uprisings.

The organizing committee consisted of Rabbi Abraham Abramowitz, Rabbi Shaul Silber, Rabbi David Graubart, Judge Harry Fisher, Max Bressler, Herman Bush, Paul Blue, Seymour Weintraub, Ralph Posner, Abe Korn, Phil Brail, Z. Tigel, Mr. and Mrs. William Weltman and Victor Rosen.

They met in Judge Harry Fisher's chambers February 25, 1944 to plan the first commemoration which took place in Orchestra Hall, May 1 of that year.

Records of these meetings and this event are sparse. They would not tell the full story if they did exist because no document could record the anger, the rage, the personal frustration and the pride the people who attended must have felt. The concentration camps were in operation and the Nazis still controlled Europe. D-Day was a month and five days off.

The commemoration, was chaired by Judge Harry Fisher. Rabbi Solomon Goldman of Anshe Emet Synagogue, as the principal speaker, stressed the single fact that "the continuity and eternal history of the Jews [are] greater than all tyrants and vile attacks on humanity put together."

The AFPJ united many of Chicago's Jewish groups to celebrate the memory of the Polish martyrs. Their memory would be celebrated, as a result, annually for fifty-three years until 1996, out of respect, pride, and a fierce determination that this extraordinary and unusual band of fighters, living or dead must be remembered. It was a commitment and at times, it was a struggle.

For many years the AFPJ was the only organization in Chicago that commemorated the Warsaw Ghetto Uprising. (In later years other groups would also have memorial meetings.) The outstanding leadership of the AFPJ included: Herman Bush, Ann Hirsch, Paul Blue, Mandel Terman, Clara and Sam Talmy, Miriam and Abe Talmy, Max Shulman, Sarah and Sol Horwitz, Phil Brail, Jack Altman, Rabbi S. Burr Yampol, Mr. and Mrs. Isadore Cutler, and Sylvia Schwartz.

The organization quickly expanded to include non-Polish Jews and, to reflect this, changed its name in 1950 to the Midwest Jewish Council. It is to the credit of the present leadership of Milton Herst, Zolman Emyanitoff, Lester Schlosberg, and the late George Landman plus all the other devoted people who spared no effort, time, or money that the Council was able to continue these memorial meetings.

Most early speakers focused on assisting the survivors. Through the years, at the Warsaw Ghetto Commemorations, when rabbis said Kaddish (prayers for the dead), the phrase "indescribable and terrible agony of millions" was repeated.

The ceremonies included a cantor singing the National Anthem and Hatikvah, a rabbi's invocation and welcoming remarks. This was followed by remarks from political and other local dignitaries. The candle lighting ceremony developed in 1982 into a beautiful annual "Passing On the Legacy" to children and grandchildren. It created an important emotional response, which was topped off with a musical or dramatic performance. The event

19

closed with singing the Partisan song, *Zog Nit Keyn Mol,* "Never say that you are going your last way."

As the years went by the various speakers included in their talks important political and social issues relevant to the problems of the day. The Warsaw Ghetto Commemoration theme, "Never Again," took on additional meaning and became an entreaty against injustice everywhere.

The rallying cry, "Never Forget" grew to include support for civil rights as well as support for Israel. Because the destruction of civil rights and civil liberties is a precursor to the politics of tyranny, the oppressed in other lands and within the United States have always been a focus of the Midwest Jewish Council. Among the specific issues with which the council dealt were immigration restrictions, racism, anti-Semitism, and the Vietnam War.

April 18, 1945
The 2nd Commemoration

The 2nd Warsaw Ghetto Commemoration, April 18, 1945 in the Hamilton Hotel, was held 12 days before Hitler's suicide and 20 days before V-E Day.

The terrible unfolding of the Holocaust was yet occurring and the full, incomprehensible details of it and the Warsaw Ghetto Uprising were still coming to light. Two major questions presented themselves: How to respond as powerfully as possible to the horror of what had been happening and how to get relief as fast as they could to the people first being released from the Nazis' concentration camps.

Jack Fishbein, editor and publisher of the *Chicago Sentinel,* delivered the memorial address. "We rededicate ourselves," he said, "to holding to the cause of preventing a repetition of the tragedy of the Ghetto. We must utilize this historic occasion to vow anew that never again will the dark forces of Nazi brutality be allowed to be unleashed against the Jewish people."

His words would be matched year after year with deeds as his publication would singularly promote and publicize the annual commemorations and, as a consequence, produce the key source for a historical record of them.

Individually and as a group, the organizers and supporters of the commemoration, raised funds, food and medical supplies for the Holocaust victims fast becoming Europe's "displaced persons."

Coinciding with the commemoration, Chicago's Blackstone Theater presented the New York Yiddish play by Jacob Ben-Ami, *The Miracle of the Warsaw Ghetto*, for one week in April. It featured the New York cast of sixty, including its stars, Bertha Gerstein and Dina Halpern.

Chapter 4

1946 and 1947
The 3rd and 4th Commemorations

1946

Rabbi Abraham E. Abramowitz chaired the 1946 Commemoration of the Uprising on April 17 at his synagogue, Albany Park Hebrew Congregation. He was a guiding light and powerful motivator in helping to institute the annual commemorations of the Warsaw Ghetto Uprising.

As was earlier noted, he served as chair of the Chicago Chapter of the American Federation of Polish Jews, the organization that sponsored them.

He would later write:

> These memorial meetings which we have been arranging annually involved super human efforts by a limited group of people and a limited number of organizations. In addition to all the technical preparations, we had to ward off the opposition of certain people who were really not interested in organizing other memorial meetings but in stifling this one.

> I hope that someday when petty rivalries will disappear and sincerity will gain the upper hand, a united Chicago Jewry will arrange meetings of the magnitude that befits such a solemn occasion.

Rabbi Abramowitz was listed in the *Chicago Jewish News* (January 6, 2000, p. 38) as among the 100 most influential of Chicago Jews of the Century.

The *News* said, "He was the spiritual leader of the Albany Park Hebrew Congregation for more than 30 years, from the 1930s to the 1960s. In the Conservative movement and Zionist leader and fund-raiser for Israel, he was known as an eloquent orator who could fill all the seats of his 1,400 seat synagogue."

The Rabbi was born in Jerusalem in 1891, and ordained in Palestine. Toward the end of his life, he emigrated back to Israel where he died in 1981. He was a well-known and respected leader in the Jewish community, lecturing for the Hebrew Union College and the College of Jewish Studies. He was also Vice-President of the Chicago Rabbinical Association and an active member of B'nai B'rith and the Chicago Zionist Organization.

The speakers at the 1946 Commemoration were Rabbi Charles F. Schulman; the Honorable Stephan Rogozinski, the Polish Consul General in Chicago; and attorney Samuel A. Hoffman.

The cantor was Louis Shalinsky of the Albany Park Congregation. Songs were by the congregation choir with Miss Llamay Handel performing as soprano. Maurice Mason recited poetry.

***

1947

Rep. Emanuel Celler, Democrat from New York, served as the principal speaker for the 4th Commemoration at the Stevens Hotel, April 13, 1947.

Celler had been the sponsor of a bill for the admission of 100,000 Jews into the U.S., urging that "America set an example for the world by relaxing its immigration laws" Deplorably, the U.S.— like most countries—had severely restricted immigration during the 1930s through the 1940s when Jews were desperately trying to escape Nazi aggression.

***

The call for unity

Let every Jewish organization in Chicago arouse itself and join the sacred cause," J.I. Fishbein had editorialized in the *Sentinel*. As early as 1945, this call became controversial.

Despite Fishbein's regular and fervent editorials in the *Sentinel*, his cry for unity fell on deaf ears. Actually, as early as 1945, the Jewish Labor Committee and the American Jewish Committee had withdrawn from the coalition sponsoring the commemorations when the Jewish Peoples Fraternal Order, a section of the International Workers Order, became a co-sponsor of the event. The departing organizations had become far more politically conservative in their nature and mission than others in the sponsoring group were.

And after the war, the AFPJ had been quick to aid Russians as well as Poles.

Less controversial was the work of the Emma Lazarus Jewish Women's Clubs, a long-time supporter of the commemorations. At this point, the group was knitting sweaters for children orphaned by the Holocaust.

Herman Bush hosted a group at his home to help plan two other AFPJ meetings. It included Jan Stanczyk, Polish Minister of Labor and Social Welfare, who told of the utter destruction of Warsaw and many surrounding villages. He spoke of the plight of the remaining 80,000 Jews, including 15,000 children who were orphaned by the war.

Bush informed the Polish representatives about a dinner planned for May 1, 1946 to inaugurate a $4 million fund-raising campaign for their repatriation. He also spoke of the plans for the thirteenth annual convention of the AFPJ. No less than 1,500 persons were expected to attend the fund-raising dinner to hear Col. Gustaw Alef, military attaché of the Polish Embassy in Washington and S. Lipshitz, president of the Federation of Jewish Partisans in Poland. Jan Stanczyk had assured them, "that the Jews remaining alive are safe and will be fully protected by the Polish government; they need to rehabilitate the industrial and commercial life of Poland."

After the Kielce pogrom in 1946, where 37 surviving Jews and four Poles were murdered, a number of Chicago organizations obtained 25,000 signatures for a resolution asking President Truman to take leadership in helping Poland to oust anti-Semites from its government.

"I could not believe it," announced Samuel A. Hoffman in a radio address. "I couldn't dream that the Poles themselves, who were enslaved by the Nazis for five years, would celebrate their liberation by imitating the mass-murdering Nazis." Hoffman was especially dismayed because he had been at Herman Bush's home when Stanczyk had uttered assurance about Jews being "safe."

It was a clear act of betrayal. Nonetheless, in 1947, 1948, and 1949, the Polish Consul and the Ambassador appeared at the commemorations.

Chapter 5

1948 and 1949
The 5th and 6th Commemorations

-- Controversy --

1948

Max Bressler, president of the Chicago branch of the AJCongress, chaired the 5th Commemoration of the Warsaw Ghetto Uprising on April 17, 1948, at the Jewish People's Institute.

It was two days before the Ghetto Memorial was unveiled in Warsaw, but the Kielce pogrom in 1946 had seriously shaken the faith and hope of many Jews as to the communist government in Poland.

Herman Bush and Max Bressler, president of the Chicago branch of the AJCongress, nevertheless, enthusiastically welcomed the Polish Ambassador Josef Winiewicz, as a speaker for the 5th Commemoration.

This act alone was capable of alienating thousands of potentially more conservative Jewish supporters across the city who saw any communist state as a threat to their own lives and possibly to the country.

"The racists and hate mongers want us to forget the tremendous sacrifices made by the Soviet people in their valiant fight against our common enemy," wrote Bush in a 1946 article appealing for kits for the Jewish Council of Russian Relief. "Remember how the Red Army surging forward like a clean spear into Berlin, the rotten heart of Nazi Germany, brought light and hope to the tortured and enslaved peoples of Europe in their darkest hour."

Bush became a point man for some of the controversy. He remained convinced of the Polish government's determination to exterminate fascism and anti-Semitism.

The issues had a long history to them, however, and would sail through further rough waters in the oppressive McCarthy era of the early 1950s.

***

Multi-group relief efforts

The American Jewish Conference, an umbrella group of a number of Jewish organizations, had been organized during the war to encourage co-operation among national Jewish groups with the goal of assisting their fellow Jews in Europe. As a consequence, the Chicago branch of the AFPJ during its annual conference Feb. 17, 1944 at the Hamilton Hotel, expanded its more local agenda and worked enthusiastically to unite the *Landsmanshaften*, (benevolent societies of people from the same *shtetl* or region), along with various societies and congregations, in order to provide assistance for the less fortunate in Europe.

Irvin H. Metzger was elected president of the Chicago branch of the AFPJ and Albert H Brown, chairman of the Administration Board. An office was opened in the Chicago Loop at 135 S. LaSalle Street in order to co-ordinate fund raising and relief activities.

Such activities included obtaining information for establishing contact with relatives still in Europe. The AFPJ soon added a Businessmen's and Professional Division, and then a Women's Division. They saw their tasks clearly.

The AFPJ Statement of Purpose follows:

We bear the responsibility for the rebirth of the Jewish people in Poland, after the present terrible catastrophe. We will create the possibilities and the future existence of a Jewish community on Polish soil where the Jewish community had lived and grew in joy and in suffering for nearly a thousand years.

27

The Chicago branch of the AFPJ was organized in 1933. By 1936, it had begun to furnish relief and economic assistance to Poland. The Federation also telegraphed instructions to branches in eighteen countries from its offices in New York, London and Tel Aviv to hold a day of protest against anti-Jewish excesses in Poland. The following year, in observation of the thirtieth anniversary of the Federation, Benjamin Winter, president, and Zelig Tygel, executive director, issued the following statement:

> With the conditions facing the Jews of Poland foremost in the minds of Americans, Jews and non-Jews alike, it is fitting that the Federation of Polish Jews in America, the first organization of its kind in the world and the organization which has the fullest confidence of the 3,500,000 Jews of Polish extraction in this country, that the most prominent of Americans interested in affairs of Jewry in general join in celebrating the 30th anniversary.

The call went out for help when, at the war's end, news about survivors started coming like a flood. Chicagoans reacted with alacrity to a cable: "About 200,000 Jews were found in the regions of Poland. Those miraculously-rescued Jews are in need of immediate help. They need food, clothes and medication in order to keep alive."

On March 19, 1945, Mayor Edward Kelly and the Consul General of the USSR addressed 2,000 delegates representing numerous Jewish organizations that were gathering supplies for the Chicago Jewish Council for Russian War Relief. Donations of clothing were the admission fee for the rally at Albany Park Hebrew Congregation organized by Rabbi Abraham E. Abramowitz, Judge Harry Fisher, Rabbi S. Felix Mendelsohn, and Herman Bush. By spring 1945, under the leadership of Solomon Jesmer, chairman of the Chicago Jewish Council for Russian War Relief, Chicago Mayor Edward Kelly, and the State Commander of the American Legion, Arthur E. Canty, joined 350 Chicago Jewish organizations in their food drive.

Rabbi Abramowitz chaired the rally. Herman Bush became co-chair of the Chicago Jewish Council for Russian War Relief, seeking one million pounds of clothing, medical and other supplies. Bush had relatives in Poland, but his many activities went well beyond the personal and into the community.

Bush, it should be noted, had become a leader in a number of groups in addition to Russian War Relief: the Mayor's Volunteers Committee, United Nations Clothing Collection, Chicago Council for American Soviet Friendship, Jewish People's Choral Society, the B'nai B'rith and the American Legion. From 1935 on, Bush had served during the time of growing Polish anti-Semitism as one of the leaders, along with Rabbi Abramowitz, in support of Polish Jews.

He dedicated himself to the Russian War Relief effort after World War II as well, collecting clothing and other materials for needy Russians. His passion for the cause helped solidify his friends. When they heard stories about the Ghetto from Bush, they mobilized and began the commemorations. He was clearly a dedicated, passionate leader of great merit.

***

1949

In January 1949, Rabbi Abramowitz was elected president of the AFPJ at the organization's annual meeting.

The 6th annual Commemoration was held May 7, 1949 in Orchestra Hall. Max Bressler, who was president of the Chicago chapter of the AJCongress and headed the Advisory Board of the AFPJ, chaired it. Rabbi Abramowitz and Herman Bush participated in a tribute to Dr. Stephen S. Wise. Cantor Mihal Kusevitsky chanted *El Mole Rachamin.*

Chapter 6

1950: The Founding and Platform of the Midwest Jewish Council, Sponsor of the Commemorations of the Warsaw Ghetto Uprising

The MJC was conceived to expand the constituency beyond that of *Landsmanschaften* and the groups directly conected to Poland. During its relief efforts over the years, AFPJ had always sought to incorporate others into its ranks. In May 16, 1950, the name, Midwest Jewish Council, was adopted. As a local organization, including non-Polish Jews among its members.

During this period, the Chicago Chapter of AFPJ continued its annual conferences.

The following is the platform and statement of purpose of the Midwest Jewish Council.

> Recognizing the need for the establishment of a permanent democratic, all-inclusive, and genuinely representative organization dedicated to the principles of full equality for American Jews, the Midwest Jewish Council was established in 1950. Its purpose is to assert, maintain and protect the political and civil rights of Jews and all other minorities as guaranteed by the United States Constitution and the Bill of Rights, the cornerstones of American democracy; and to enhance and stimulate the cultural heritage of the Jewish people.

> The Midwest Jewish Council is therefore established as a vehicle through which all Jews, regardless of their political affiliation, can council and reason together in a democratic spirit, thus arriving at a program best suited for the advancement of the aforementioned needs and goals.

Platform

1. To combat the growth of racism and anti-Semitism by exposing them to the public view and mobilizing public opinion against them.

2. To fight all trends toward thought control and Hitler-like hysteria. As Americans devoted to the preservation of basic rights, we believe that democracy is weakened by subverting its traditional guarantees and safeguards.

3. To do everything possible to maintain the State of Israel as a free, democratic and independent Jewish nation.

4. To do all we can to promote the development of Jewish cultural values through forums, concerts, choral groups, films, art exhibits, and all other means at our disposal.

5. To forever commemorate, by meetings and other means, the mass slaughter of the Jewish People of Europe along with the destruction of their homes and cities. By thus commemorating the Holocaust, American peace-loving people may be reminded of the catastrophic results of hate, and thereby be assured that such atrocities will never be repeated upon the face of the earth.

Chapter 7

Herman Bush:
President, The Midwest Jewish Council
1950-1971

His Heritage

Herman Bush had been elected president of AFPJ in 1945 and served in this post until 1949. In 1950, he became president of the Midwest Jewish Council, a position he held until his death, in 1971.

Members from the early days of the MJC remember Bush as a successful businessman, a dedicated Jew, a staunch liberal who raised millions of dollars for Israel, and a man of true leadership.

At the end of the 1945 meeting, Bush had read a letter from his son, who was serving in the U.S. Army, stationed in Germany. The young soldier wrote of his visit to a camp where 40 Jews, mostly Hungarians and Czechoslovakians, were still hungry.

The response was swift. A campaign committee, chaired by Philip Pinkwater, collected 25,000 emergency food and medicine kits. "Let's give till it hurts," had proclaimed an editorial in *The Sentinel.* "Each kit cost four dollars and contained shortening, sugar, condensed milk, cocoa, farina, fruit extract, chocolate, soap and medical supplies. These ordinary household items which we take for granted can actually save lives."

The Chicago branch of the AJCongress, the Jewish National Worker's Alliance, Labor Zionists and Hadassah called upon all their branches to cooperate with the AFPJ relief campaigns. Under the leadership of Mrs. Solomon L. Zax, who launched the Women's Kit Campaign, volunteers picked up clothing anywhere in the city and brought them to one of thirty-four stations. She had appealed to all Chicago women's organizations, exhorting them to "join together and free them, the war victims, from further terror."

"We dare not fail," Mrs. Zax proclaimed. "We cannot take time off to weep. There is work to be done so that the survivors may be rescued not only physically but spiritually as well."

Women were also active on political fronts. They urged President Truman, the U.S. Congress and the entire Illinois congressional delegation to open U.S. doors to refugees from Nazi Germany. While appealing to have Israel recognized as a state (most U.S political leaders were reluctant to do so at that time), women's groups demanded that "the British Government open up the gates of Palestine immediately, and admit the homeless victims of the Nazis' monstrous crimes and fulfill their obligation that Palestine become a Jewish National Home."

The women's organizations began raising funds for the new state. Other resolutions protested to the French government "for refusing to return the surviving Jewish children to the Jewish Agency."

Delegates from Jewish organizations pledged to raise $300,000 to support the publication of the *Black Book*, a compilation of the names of people who had died in the Holocaust. Max Bressler, president of the Chicago division of the AJCongress, chaired the *Black Book* campaign in Chicago.

University of Chicago Professor Oscar R. Lange, a Catholic educator who had visited the Soviet Union and spoken with Joseph Stalin, was a major speaker at several fund-raising rallies held at the Albany Park Hebrew Congregation. Journalist Zelig Yygel, representing the national AFPJ, spoke about the Jews in Poland during a meeting chaired by a group of prominent rabbis headed by Moses Eichenstein of the Austrian-Galician Synagogue.

In June 1945, about 500 delegates and others, many representing societies bearing the names of their hometowns in Poland, attended the twelfth annual convention of the Chicago district of the AFPJ. Abe Korn, chairman, opened the convention. In the keynote address, Albert Brown, chair of administration, emphasized that the main interest of the convention was "to create possibilities for practical deeds to help the suffering Jews who remained alive in Poland and those Jews hailing from Poland who are now scattered in various parts of Europe."

Thus, for a special but brief period of time, immediately after the war, Jewish organizations were allied for the pursuit of two goals: first, to help with the relief effort for their fellow Jews; and second, to commemorate the Warsaw Ghetto Uprising

The next year, on April 21, 1946, at the Jewish Music Festival, Eugene Malek conducted the orchestra, and world-renown cantor and tenor Richard Tucker starred with a 100-voice choir at the Civic Opera House. The festival celebrated 100 years of Jewish communal life in Chicago. Bush was eloquent as he expressed his joy in the music:

"A great moral responsibility has fallen to us, the Americans of Jewish faith, to preserve and enhance our great heritage of Jewish culture which was nearly wiped out. We in Chicago especially are called upon to fulfill this duty and privilege. The success of this event will stimulate Jewish communities in all parts of the United States to encourage talented artists and musicians to take up the task of preserving for the world the great Jewish contributions to the culture of the world."

Still in 1946, concern intensified for Polish Jews remaining in Russia and other war survivors unable to find places to live outside of detention camps. Plans to resettle displaced refugees were explained in AFPJ fund-raising dinners with a distinguished list of guest speakers: Polish Consul Honorable Jan Galewicz, a Jew; Dr. Emil Sommerstein, chairman of the Jewish Central Committee in Poland; and Bertram W. Korn, Hebrew Associations of Peiping, Tientsin and Tsingtao.

Mrs. Herman Bush, working through the Women's Division of the American Jewish Conference, collected food, medicine, and clothing. She also inaugurated the "Save a Child" program to encourage the adoption of Polish Jewish orphans. The annual upkeep of one child was $300 at that time. The women's group also contributed to the maintenance of Hebrew schools in Lodz and other Polish cities and supported the resettlement of orphans in Birobidzhan.

Chapter 8

Co-operation and Division

Clearly, the effort to work with other organizations was always an item on the agenda of the Midwest Jewish Council.

Early on, all Chicago Jewish organizations were asked to send representatives to hear Sidney Flatow, executive director of the AFPJ, and former UNRRA (United Nations Relief and Rehabilitation Administration) administrator for displaced persons. Zionist leader Samuel Hoffman joined him in a concerted call for unity.

Affairs within groups and organizations, however, can become rocky. They did not, nor do they always, go smoothly. Jewish groups are much like many others. Even the important act of commemorating the martyrs became a source of conflict.

An understanding of the history of Jewish migration to the U.S. helps to explain some of the social and political divisions The *JUF NEWS,* January 2000, tells a brief story of Jewish immigration to the U.S. The headline read: "German Jews were the largest segment of the early Chicago Jewish community."

"The typical German Jew," wrote Rabbi Morris Gutstein of Congregation. Shaare Tikvah in *A Priceless Heritage*, "considered German his vernacular, read German newspapers, attended German theater and built his social life on German patterns."

While a few members of the Eastern European Jewish community made the leap from peddling to industrialist or financier, the majority settled into running small dry-goods and clothing stores and working in the trades. Some small businessmen became grocery storeowners or drycleaning and tailoring operators. Still others made it to college and became professionals. Many who attained affluence helped mold the community's charitable structure and assisted new arrivals in gaining a financial foothold on an individual basis.

The flow to large metropolitan areas was probably influenced by the fact that most East European Jews had lived in more crowded communities than Western European Jews had, and their career choices were more city-oriented than town-to-town peddling. The influx of Jews from Eastern Europe to Chicago led to the formation of *landsmanshaften.* Between the Eastern and Western Jews in Europe, there were and are many cultural, social, educational, professional and religious differences..

Throughout the city, organizations were formed to promote professional, social economic and political ends. The Jews coming from Europe, especially from Germany before the turn of the twentieth century, had established their lives and their businesses or careers, often with significant financial success. Others mainly from Russia, Lithuania, and Poland had immigrated more recently and were considered the newcomers on the block. The recent arrivals spoke Yiddish, the mother tongue of the Eastern European Jews, or spoke English with distinct accents that made them stand out as "foreigners."

They were less assimilated into the mainstream of American culture than were the German Jews. They held on tightly to the customs of the Old World, ate traditional meals, tended to live within identified communities. There were vested interests to protect and self-interest to promote. And yes, there was a social hierarchy that translated into snobbery.

The countless Jewish organizations in the U.S. represented the vast breadth of the Jewish population. Despite a solid history of Jewish philanthropy, it did not take long before the various groups within the Jewish community became divided. The call for unity was disregarded.

Three delegates from the Jewish Peoples Fraternal Order section of the International Workers Order (rumored to be a Communist front organization) including H.B. Ritman, prominent Chicago attorney and president of the Chicago JPFO, had been admitted to membership in the American Jewish Conference meeting in New York.

Citing this decision, (in effect saying, "We won't work with them.") the Jewish Labor Committee and the American Jewish Committee withdrew from the Conference. Consequently, the American Jewish Committee and the Jewish Labor Committee planned a separate fund-raising effort to fight anti-Semitism and rebuild Jewish culture overseas.

Chapter 9

McCarthyism Creates a Split in the Chicago Jewish Community

Starting in 1951, two Warsaw Ghetto Commemorations reflecting the political split within the city, would be held in Chicago.

The split was generated to a large extent by McCarthyism and the spirit of fear on which it nourished. Despite the competition, or perhaps because of it, attendance that year exceeded expectations.

"More than 1,800 people crowded the Grand Ballroom of the Sherman Hotel. It was the most successful Warsaw Ghetto Uprising Commemorastion ever held in the city of Chicago," The *Sentinel* wrote. "The large audience amazed experienced observers in view of the deliberate attempts by traditional enemies of unity in Jewish life to prevent a large turnout."

The history of the Midwest Jewish Council is not unique to this time period in the United States. Dissension has never been unusual. Even in the Warsaw Ghetto, where ultimate unity of purpose forged a coalition of heroic proportions, many Jews demonstrated behavior that indicated a loyalty to nothing else but raw survival.

Some Jews in the Ghetto became foremen of the slave laborers; others became police officers, working with the Germans to round up and attack their fellow Jews. They did so often out of a deluded and vain effort at preserving themselves and their families for as long as possible. Many within this group were caught up in a tragic desire to enhance their own status at the expense of their fellow man.

Others were blackmailed into doing the work, having been threatened that if they did not work with the enemy, their own families would be at risk. They turned against their fellow Jews and were thus able to steel themselves even amidst the pleas of their former neighbors and friends who were forced onto the death-awaiting cattle cars. Ironically, the turncoats who made up the *Judenrat* or

Jewish Council were murdered as well, just as soon as they proved to be no longer useful to the Nazis.

The 1950s were bringing changes both within the AFPJ and in its relationships with other organizations. In America, during this period, Jewish groups became deeply divided along political and social lines.

The attitudes of Jewish groups toward one another sometimes grew hostile, divisive and acrimonious. This continued for years until most Jewish people of all political and social stripes finally felt safe enough to see the truth and accept the annual commemorations.

Many within the AFPJ were decidedly left-of-center. Like any number of the leaders within the Ghetto Uprising, most of its membership were tradesmen and came from unions. Some owned small businesses. Others were very successful businessmen and women or professionals, but all were decidedly politically progressive. They showed a deep sense of responsibility towards their fellows along with a commitment to fight for social justice. Staunch civil libertarians and sympathizers with workers everywhere, their politics ranged from liberal to decidedly socialistic.

Washington-based correspondent Milton Friedman in October 1950 asked, "Are Jewish organizations succumbing to 'Commiphobia?'" He was referring to the Jewish community's response to a *Chicago Tribune* article written by Walter Trohan equating communism and zionism. Herman Bush subsequently condemned the Jewish leaders who met with the *Tribune* editors without contacting key Chicago people or developing consensus on the *Tribune's* position. "The agencies should have demanded a retraction of the statements made in Mr. Trohan's article," he said.

The Jewish community found itself divided over issues that pulled asunder different groups in a number of different directions. Within this myriad of Jewish organizations, groups were not immune to clashes over American communism, especially during the 1950s when the House Un-American Activities Committee (HUAC) investigated many "liberal" individuals and organizations. McCarthyism became a major force dividing Americans into camps.

Significantly, the AFPJ was absent from a testimonial dinner in January 1951 honoring Max Bressler for his work as president of the Zionist Organization of Chicago. This might have been the result of several years of conflict. On one hand there were Chicago leaders who understood that AFPJ did not want to jeopardize Bressler's position as a leader of AJCongress.

The *Sentinel* had reported May 5, 1947 that the AJCongress had responded to a vicious campaign of character assassination launched against it for its refusal to join the current anti-Communist and anti-Soviet hysteria. The article referred to the AJCongress Journal and praised the Chicago branch for its position.

Bush joined with a group of Chicago Jewish leaders in denouncing the anti-immigration Walter-McCarran Bill in Congress "as racist and discriminatory and as constituting a threat to civil rights in the United States." These are the same civil liberties that the MJC has worked tirelessly to protect.

In March 1953, the split had become painful and name-calling had begun. In response, Rabbi Abramowitz wrote a forceful open letter to David F. Silverzweig, then President of the AJCongress in Chicago. He outlined his position that "using smear tactics of the lowest form is endangering Jewish leadership, Jewish organizations and more than anything else, independence of thought on the part of public-spirited and social-minded individuals."

The rabbi was extremely upset over what he called the "puerile conflict" seen in the behavior of the two different communities planning the Warsaw Ghetto Uprising Commemorations.

Every year, he wrote, the AFPJ leadership "summoned all organizations in the city to participate, never imposing a program, but always abiding by the decision of the committees appointed by the respective preliminary conferences. During some of these years other organizations also arranged memorial meetings. No one doubted that the AFPJ has a right to sponsor meetings. But Mr. Bush's request for a meeting with Mr. Silverzweig was rejected."

Rabbi Abramowitz challenged the AJCongress and sent a letter asking, "Why was it necessary to send speakers to various groups asking them to boycott the American Federation of Polish Jews' Memorial Meeting? I am sure that the gentlemen of your

Board realize how ridiculous is the accusation that the Federation is a 'communist front organization, or that any one of its leaders are 'subversive.'"

While the vicious campaign against himself and against the AFPJ prompted the detailed letter, the rabbi wrote in defense of Herman Bush: "It is the smears and character assassination directed against Mr. Herman Bush that grieves and chagrins me. I have known Mr. Bush for twenty-five years, and I admire his social-mindedness, his charity-mindedness, his Jewish-mindedness, and his patriotism. I do not claim that he is the greatest man in this community, but I will say without hesitation, that he is the most active man in this community.

"Whenever and wherever work was needed and personal sacrifices in money, time or effort were called for, Mr. Bush was always ready to assume responsibility."

Rabbi Abramowitz noted the many times Bush worked with the AJCongress and for Israel bonds when he was not as alleged a "fellow-traveler."

"How long ago was it that you, the officers and leaders of the Congress asked Mr. Bush to serve as your delegate to the World Jewish Congress in Geneva?" he asked.

In an ultimate attempt at a put-down, Mr. Silverzweig replied to the Rabbi's letter, "…there are not (emphasis added) two committees representing confederations of organizations. There is but one such committee, brought into being by the AJCongress and the Congress for Jewish Culture." Then he listed thirty-one organizations, including the Associated Talmud Torahs, B'nai B'rith, the rabbinical associations, and labor organizations. And he concluded, "We have no doubt that the Federation (AFPJ) was a meaningful and reputable organization prior to 1943. Since that time, however,…this organization has been reduced to a shell."

While the *Sentinel* did not report on the *other* memorial, it did take note that the MJC commemoration in 1953 attracted 2,000 people at the Sherman Hotel. Despite the animosity over the staging of two separate commemorative events, a letter from an unknown writer to the *Sentinel* indicated something good was going on. The event "made him proud to be a Jew," the author wrote.

The following year, Jack Fishbein again pleaded for a united, dignified memorial under the auspices of the entire Chicago Jewish community. The pleas did nothing to unify anyone. Separate commemorations continued under the sponsorship of the MJC and would continue annually until 1996

No sadder indication of this division exists than in the story of Rabbi Ira Eisenstein of Anshe Emet Synagogue. Eisenstein was a newcomer to Chicago. When he received two invitations to speak he asked, "Are there two meetings?"

The answer came from one group: "Those are a bunch of communists."

The answer from the other group: "They are just a bunch of McCarthyites."

Then the Rabbi asked himself, "How are we honoring the Warsaw Ghetto fighters by permitting them to become the pawns of an internecine feud?" He declined both invitations

The acrimony continued. Within the Spertus Institute archives can be found an AJCongress paper dated March 16, 1956.

Labeled, "Urgent," the paper reveals a letter to the Anti-Defamation League: "...so-called 'Midwest Jewish Council' is arranging a meeting on April 15. I am taking the liberty of asking you to urge your membership *not* to participate...."

At a meeting of the Chicagoland Jewish Organizations convened by the AJCongress on January 2, 1957, Rabbi Fox proposed to write Herman Bush a letter asking for a list of organizations making up the MJC. While the rabbi's motive for this proposal is unclear, the effort was tabled.

It was a challenging time for the Jewish community. Although individual synagogues had sponsored commemorations, not until 1951 did a competing group actually sponsor a separate citywide commemoration.

The Chicago Yiskor Committee for Six Million Martyrs had taken its name in 1957. It consisted of thirty-one organizations including the Associated Talmud Torahs, B'nai B'rith, and the Rabbinical Associations. The Yiskor Committee called the Midwest Jewish Council (MJC) "communist sympathizers."

The former AFPJ had tried unsuccessfully to bring about a unified commemoration. Separate memorials reflected deep political, cultural and religious division within the Chicago Jewish community.

Organizational discord, however, continued and grew international in scope. This is indicated in the minutes of a 1957 meeting in Warsaw of Israeli trade union leaders, along with the Central Council of Cultural-Social Association of Polish Jews. They also show that a "question was raised of the possibility of resuming contacts between the Association of Polish Jews and the World Jewish Congress."

The same year, the Jewish Telegraph Agency reported from London, depicting mass requests for emigration by Poland's Jews. It confirmed the concern that "Polish excesses were more extensive than previously rumored." Translation: "There was more trouble for Jewish people in Poland and the desire to leave the country became an urgent need."

It became apparent that Herman Bush's dream and efforts for the rehabilitation of a free Poland had proved futile. On the other hand, his dream to keep the story of the Uprising alive was inspiring commemorations in nearly forty nations throughout the world.

Chapter 10

The Red Squad

From 1955 to 1969, the Chicago Police Red Squad zealously kept a file on the MJC and designated the group as a "communist-infiltrated organization." The MJC was in good company. The PTA, the League of Women Voters, and 76 other community organizations had been listed as Red Squad targets.

The police unit was supposedly established to monitor "subversive activities," but as inevitably happens with monitors who have such vague and unlimited authority, its definition of the term and its methods turned into an attack on the liberties it was supposed to be defending. The squad's files would eventually become public, but little would be known or understood about the unjust damage the monitoring caused to individuals and to causes.

Endless pages of compiled reports by the Chicago Red Squad were in the possession of the Police Department and were obtained by Richard Gutman, attorney for the American Civil Liberties Union in 1976. Gutman later became the attorney for the Bill of Rights Foundation and worked on other civil rights challenges.

The file, containing information on the MJC, revealed that a number of Memorial attendees were listed as "communist" or "fellow travelers." Names of specific individuals were included. Of course, those who spied at the commemorations heard nothing treasonous, but they did have an opportunity to learn a great deal about the Holocaust.

Frank Donner's 1990 book, *Protectors of Privilege: Red Squads and Police Repression in Urban America,* describes how seemingly enthusiastic infiltrators successfully became involved and accepted in the activities of a number of radical or progressive groups. These included Women Strike for Peace, the Democratic Party of Evanston, the Vietnam Veterans Against the War, Teachers for Radical Change in Education, and the Midwest Jewish Council.

In the fall of 1977, one infiltrator, Sheli Lulkin, was exposed in the course of litigation. For years, however, she had become quite successful at supplying the police with mailing lists of her targets.

Donner wrote, "The ecumenical range of Lulkin's targets even included a meeting on April 20, 1968, of the MJC in memory of victims of the Warsaw Ghetto massacre. She characterized the Council as 'pinkish' because it has always been anti-Israel and anti-Zionist. Lulkin does not understand or recognize the use of the Yiddish and Hebrew languages."

The principal speaker, on whom she reported was Congressman Abner Mikva (D. IL) who "urged support of the fight for black rights."

Eventually, after successful legal challenges, the Red Squad in Chicago was finally disbanded. During 1998, however, under Mayor Richard M. Daley's leadership, another effort was made to revive a version of the Red Squad. This time, the approach was couched as an anti-gang effort, but the methods and goals were similar—spying and infiltration. Again, Attorney Rick Gutman helped to lead the legal challenge. The Mayor, forever persistent, sent the Corporation Counsel back to the drawing board for yet another rewrite of the law.

A major event that brought the MJC under surveillance by the Chicago Police Department's Red Squad was a tribute dinner in memory of Dr. Albert Einstein, which took place on December 4, 1955.

Many within the Jewish establishment, even after the files became public, remained silent at this assault on the people's right to gather. Their reasons ranged from protecting their own hard-won established positions of personal, financial and political success to a genuine fear of the communist threat to their way of life. Whatever their motivation, they failed to see the insidious effects of their failure to protest the Red Squad's involvement.

And seldom were the results clearer than in the Midwest Jewish Council's attempt to honor Einstein. At the tribute to him, Bush announced a scholarship for Jewish students in scientific studies. Rabbi Abramowitz and Paul Arthur Schilpp, professor of philosophy at Northwestern University, spoke on Einstein's contributions to the world. Ben Aronin had written a play for the occasion called *The Stars Can Wait,* featuring Cantor Moses Silverman along with composer and concert artist Erwin Jospe.

It is not clear whether disapproval was for Einstein or the MJC or both, but it is important to note the fact that Einstein was considered a "fellow-traveler" by some at the same time and therefore those persons did not consider it a good idea at all to arrange such a memorial affair.

"I myself have been called a 'leftist' and let me tell you that if one has to be a leftist to arrange an Einstein Memorial affair, then I am certainly one," Herman Bush wrote at the time.

It was with irony and pride at the end of 1999 that MJC participants noted that Albert Einstein was chosen by *Time Magazine* as "The Person of the Century." His wise and thoughtful face graced the magazine's cover. Forty-four years earlier, for their vision, the Council's leaders were suspect.

Chapter 11

The Early 1950s Brings New Energy to the Commemorations

Those who organized the Warsaw Ghetto Commemorations in Chicago saw programs in memory of the Holocaust as well as the Warsaw Ghetto Uprising start to spread internationally.

In Europe, Israel and the United States, collective Remembrance Days, for example, were becoming far more common. In Warsaw, on such occasions, large crowds would gather around the monument of the Ghetto fighters as the Uprising there was seen more and more not only as sharply painful history but also as a symbol of martyrdom, heroism and resistance.

More and more during these early days, a growing focus became an additional part of the commemorations. Increasingly, people brought their children, grandchildren and other young people to hear their stories as well as the accounts of others.

For more than fifty years, young and old, would join together in shouting, "Never again." As a result of such a spirit on the part of the participants, Chicago's Warsaw Ghetto Uprising Commemoraions witnessed increased interest. At the same time, the introduction of spirited, well-crafted dramatic performances and tough, pointed commentary by the speakers added further excitement to the events.

Again, Herman Bush became the person who helped to focus the organization and its programs. He understood the U.S. mentality. Political issues always played a major role within the MJC.

"The commemorations," he wrote at this time, "are proving beyond doubt the necessity of further discussion and plans for action in order to rid the world of a corruption, which will surely thrive as long as there is so much indifference among our Jewish leaders."

Many well-established American Jews, he argued, were interested in denying the scope of the Holocaust. Others continued to remain in other levels of denial, convinced that "it wasn't that bad," until it became "safe" or "fashionable" many years later to join in the official commemorations.

***

1950

The 7th Commemoration was held April 15, 1950 at the Midland Hotel. Its dramatic presentation was contributed by Vivian Goldstein.

Speaker James Waterman Wise, director of the Council Against Intolerance in America, spoke with the kind of strong, focused commentary that those who participated were beginning to expect as part of the commemorations. Still, Wise shocked his audience by describing the Nuremberg trials of the German war criminals as a farce. Germany, he believed, was being re-Nazified.

***

1951

At the 8th Commemoration held April 29, 1951 at the Sherman Hotel, Keith Wheeler, a war correspondent for the *Chicago Sun-Times*, was the featured speaker. His comments added coals to the troubling theory espoused a year earlier by Wise. Wheeler, the author of several novels outlined in a scholarly manner the danger of the present attempt to re-Nazify Germany.

Ann Hirsch (at the time, Mrs. Oscar Moskowitz) started her long association with MJC in the 1951 candle-lighting ceremony. She would subsequently serve the Midwest Jewish Council as president from 1971 to 1983.

Ann Hirsch (1895-1991), widowed four times, was the mother of three daughters. A long-time legal secretary and court reporter, she remained according to her daughter Shirley Gale--

a vital and vibrant woman into her 90s. Mrs. Gale remembers her mother as a deeply-involved woman.

"She had a career well before most women even considered working outside the home," her daughter recalled. "She was well-read, well-traveled, intensely invested in her causes and was a spine of strength. In addition to her total support for Israel, Mrs. Hirsch first became involved with MJC as a representative of the Mizrachi Women and the National Council of Jewish Women. She took on leadership roles for a very long time."

***

1952

On April 26, 1952, the 9th Commemoration was also held at the Sherman Hotel, with S. B. Komaiko, Rabbi Abramowitz and J. Fishbein as speakers.

The occasion was noteworthy for the initial performance of the *Megillah of the Warsaw Ghetto* by Ben Aronin. Rosylin Harvey signed it for the hard-of-hearing.

Ben Aronin, according to the *Chicago Jewish News,* was "an educator, writer and composer, was on the faculties of Anshe Emet Synagogue and the College of Jewish Studies for many years. He also wrote and directed many Jewish pageants, Purim plays, and radio and television scripts."

These programs, along with outstanding speakers, not only remembered the Warsaw Ghetto martyrs, but also associated them with other persecuted groups as well. Aronin was listed in the same issue of the *Chicago Jewish News* (January 6, 2000), as one of the 100 most influential Jews of the past century.

"Megillah of the Warsaw Ghetto" by Ben Aronin
(Performed April 26, 1952, and April 4, 1953, at the
9th and 10th Commemorations)
Before the Nazi wave of horror swept over Poland

Quenching the lives of its three million Jews, there dwelt in Warsaw a Jewish community numbering half a million.

In November 1939, the Nazis set up a Ghetto surrounded by barbed wire
And there imprisoned Warsaw's Jews.
On July 22, 1942, the Nazis asked the Jewish Concil to supply them each day with 6,000 to 10,000 prisoners
To be evacuated, as they said, to "better places."
In the months that followed, it became clear
That the thousands upon thousands of Jewish men, women and children
Who had relied upon the Nazi promise
Had been marched into the gas chambers and crematories of Treblinka.

On December 1, 1942, the once proud city of Warsaw
Numbered only forty thousand Jews.
Cartloads of dead Jewish children
Rumbled heavily over the pavements
And corpses lay unburied on the sidewalks.
On December 15, 1942, the Jews resolved to launch an armed revolt
Against the Nazi hordes.
Tunnels were dug, crude hand grenades were made.
Rifles, clubs and iron tools were distributed as weapons.
On April 19, 1943, the first day of Passover,
The revolt began....
The Nazis, having lost more than twelve hundred troops
In their assaults upon the Ghetto
Dropped thousands of incendiary bombs from planes
In an attempt to burn the Ghetto to the ground.

From the burning hell of the Warsaw Ghetto
The Jewish fighters sent this message
To their fellow Polish citizens
Outside the Ghetto walls:

"POLES CITIZENS, SOLDIERS FOR FREEDOM! FROM UNDER THE POUNDING OF THE GERMAN CANNONS WHICH THE GERMAN ARMY IS HAMMERING AGAINST OUR HOUSES,THE HOMES OF OUR MOTHERS, WIVES AND CHILDREN,FROM UNDER THE FLAME OF MACHINE GUNS WHICH WE HAVE CAPTURED FROM THE COWARDLY GERMAN ENEMY,FROM UNDER THE SMOKE AND THE BLOOD OF THE MURDERED WARSAW GHETTO,WE SEND YOU GREEETINGS.
EACH THRESHOLD IN THE GHETTO HAS BEEN AND WILL CONTINUE TO BE A STRONGHOLD.
WE MAY ALL DIE IN THIS BATTLE BUT WE WILL NOT SURRENDER!"
They fell, every man, woman and child—defying the massed tanks. Heavy artillery and gas attacks of the murderous foe.
They died that liberty might live!
They died that Israel might live!
They died that you and I might live!
Blessed be their memory forever!

Early in 1952, Herman Bush and Rabbi Abramowitz led a petition campaign organized by sixty-seven Chicago groups to protest Jewish negotiations for the reparations with Germany. "Shall we remain silent while a sellout is being engineered? Shall we accept blood money from Nazi butchers?"

They were particularly aghast by the prospect of ex-Nazis eligible for immigration while Jewish immigration restrictions continued. The AFPJ supported a bill introduced by Reps. Herbert

Lehman. (D-NY) and Emanuel Celler. The bill would encourage immigration of 100,000 wartime victims.

***

1953

As previously mentioned, the tenth annual Warsaw Ghetto Uprising Commemoration, in 1953 proved an unprecedented success, with 2,000 in attendance at the Sherman Hotel, a fact noted by *The Sentinel.*

Despite the fact that the planning was fraught with conflict, Jews from every section of the city filled the Grand Ballroom and the balcony to overflowing in a mighty demonstration that Chicago Jewry would not easily forget.

Rabbi Abramowitz and Samuel A. Hoffman, vice president of the Exchange National Bank and former Assistant States Attorney, were designated the main speakers.

Ben Aronin's *The Megillah of the Warsaw Ghetto* was repeated, this time with Pearl Harand doing a hand-signing interpretation.

***

1954

The 11th Commemoration of the Warsaw Ghetto Uprising was moved to the Palmer House on April 10, 1954. Speakers were Rabbi A.E. Abramowitz and Samuel A. Hoffman. The organizing committee in preparation for it had reached out to the whole region by inviting representatives of 500 organizations to planning meetings.

Preparations for the commemoration, that year and also the one in 1955 fell under the auspices of a citywide committee.

51

Chapter 12

1955 to 1963

Along New Faces the Dramatic Scripts of Ben Aronin

Many committed Jews worked hard to keep the commemorations going and vital. To list all the names and events becomes impossible. Some leaders and what they accomplished, however, are important to note and remember.

The commemorations by other organization were different because the programs did not regularly include guest speakers who talked about critical political issues. The candle-lighting ceremony was always dramatic and poignant. The commemorations then closed with the singing of the Hymn of the Partisan: *Zog Nit Keyn Mol.*

Over the years, many rabbis and cantors participated in various ways, making the annual commemorations a regular part of their lives. Rabbi Abramowitz was joined by Rabbis S. Burr Yampol, Chair of the Anti-Nazi Committee; Malcolm Cohn, of Temple B'nai Yehuda; Manahim M. Goodman of Congregation Anshe Motele; Ernst M. Lorge Temple Beth Israel; Robert Marx of Congregation Hakafa.

Among the cantors and soloists were: Harold Brindel, of Temple Har Zion; Moses Silverman of Congregation Anshe Emet; Pavel Slavensky, former member of the Belgrade Royal Opera Company; David Politzer of Temple Menorah; Shlomo Shuster, Niles Township Congregation; Hasha Musha, cantorial soloist and Klezmer singer and soloist Laurie Sucher.

A number of talented people took part in the presentation of original scripts written by Ben Aronin and others during the years 1952 to 1963. Despite a boycott of the commemorations by a number of organizations, outstanding talent with national reputations contributed to these events. They came because they realized the significance of the commemorations starting with

Howard DaSilva and Jacob Ben-Ami, stars from "The World of Sholom Aleichem," who had dramatized the historic uprising at the 1954 Commemoration.

***

1955

The 12th Annual Commemoration was held April 17 at the Palmer House. Rabbi Abramowitz spoke and Rabbi Aaron Rine from Congregation Beth Yitzchok gave the invocation.

A group led by Cantor Moses Silverman of Anshe Emet and the talented and well-known violinist, Elaine Skorodin presented Aronin's script, "These We Remember." This year marked the beginning of Sonya Kass accompanying the cantor on the piano.

***

1956

On April 15, again meeting at the Palmer House, the commemoration attendees heard Ann Laskin and Rabbi Abramowitz as speakers.

Actor Everett Clarke portrayed the main character in the dramatic presentation of "The Trial of Peter Schultz" by Ben Aronin. It dealt with an indictment against a German accused of murdering Jews.

***

1957

Those who participated in or attended the April 7 Commemoration at the Palmer House heard Everett Clarke read

Aronin's script, "From Mourning to Morning." It was a powerful presentation with a poignant local connection as it was the story of Johanna Starkopf, a 16-year- old Von Steuben High School student who had been smuggled from the Ghetto in a coffin at the age of 18 months.

The speaker was historian and columnist Ben Zion Goldberg.

***

1958

The commemoration held April 7, 1958 at the Sherman Hotel was the 15th annual one held in Chicago. Studs Terkel, dressed in a trench coat, marked it by narrating Ben Aronin's play, "The Great Hour." Everett Clarke portrayed the main character, Shamai the Tailor. He whispered, "Wiederstand, resist!" during the chanting of the Kaddish at the synagogue. It was the signal to fight. "When a bullet hit Shamai on the fifth day, with his last breath," he called out to the others, "Wiederstand, resist!"

Cantor Pavel Slavensky along with sisters Sulie and Pearl Harand (known for their very successful drama school in the Chicago area) played roles. The Harands would become regular performers at the commemorations.

Herman Bush's niece, Ciporah Fox, lit one of the six memorial candles in memory of her parents. They were "liquidated by the Nazis" when she was but three years old. Bush had worked for seven years before he was able to bring his niece to the United States.

Miss Fox at the time of the commemoration was a nursing student at Cook County Hospital and a student at Wright Junior College. She had escaped first to Hungary, and later to Israel before coming to the United States.

She spoke at the commemoration telling her story.

"My mother was shot as we ran for the hills, and my father was not strong enough to live through our months in the cave," she said.

Her survival was possible because the group "subsisted" for 22 months "on whatever game they could trap and a few potatoes" that a Polish farmer would leave in secret places.

***

1959

The 16th annual Commemoration of the Warsaw Ghetto Uprising was held April 6, 1959 at the Palmer House. The Halevi Choral Society, directed by Hyman Reznick, sang Aronin's "We Hear Their Voices." The speakers were Rabbi Carl Richter of Sinai Temple in Michigan City, Indiana, and Rabbi Abramowitz.

***

1960

At the 17th annual Commemoration of the Warsaw Ghetto Uprising on April 17, 1960 the speakers were Senator Stephen M. Young of Ohio; the Honorable Stefan Rogozinski, Poland's Consul General for Chicago; and businessman Mandel Terman. It was held at the Palmer House. Aronin's 1960 play, "And Still They March,' was dramatized by Everett Clarke and Morris Carnowksy.

***

1961

On April 1961, the 18th Commemoration was also held at the Palmer House. The speakers were Senator Wayne Morse of Oregon,

Rabbi Abramowitz and Gerry Revzin. A Yiddish segment was added to the program at this time and from 1961 to 1995 Ms. Revzin made conducting it her specialty. The significance of this addition was underlined by the fact that Yiddish represented the mother tongue of most of the Warsaw fighters.

Israel was preparing at the time for the trial of Adolf Eichmann, architecht of "the final solution." Accordingly, Aronin wrote "Eichmann's Accomplices," in which famed actor Howard DaSilva played the role of the prosecutor. DaSilva's character expressed the drama's thesis in the lines: "the only ones who showed the courage to rise up and resist, knowing definitely that their fate of doom is sealed, only those are not guilty of being accomplices."

***

1962

On April 15, 1962, the 19th Commemoration was held at McCormick Place. The speakers were Maryland Gov. Theodore Mckedlin and U.S. federal court Judge Abraham Lincoln Marovitz

Aronin's, "Epic of the Warsaw Ghetto" was performed as was Eugene Yevtushenko's "Babi Yar," starring Everett Clarke, Cantor Moses Silverman, Dee Clark, Gil Poldolner, Barbara Dombre, John Tibbs, and Peter Irmeter.

***

1963

The 20th Commemoration of the Warsaw Ghetto Uprising ceremony was held April 7, 1963 at the Sherman House hotel. Threats were made by the American Nazi Party that its members would picket the event. A telegram was sent to the Mayor's office requesting police protection for the memorial at the Sherman House Hotel. The Nazis did not show.

Senator Stephen M. Young of Ohio, author Sidney Lens, Rabbi S. Burr Yampol and Rabbi Abramowitz were the speakers.

Sidney Lens, a well-respected, progressive leader in his union, the United Service Employees, AFL-CIO "proposed nuclear disarmament and a peaceful approach to the world's problems."

Rabbi S. Burr Yampol (1899-1969) was chair of the National Committee to Combat Nazism. He was on the program many years from 1958 to 1967, having received an encouraging letter from President Eisenhower to continue his work exposing Nazi activities.

Rabbi Yampol was the leader of the Chicago Anti-Heusinger Committee. Heusinger was an identified Nazi war criminal. As chair, however, of the permanent military committee of NATO, he was protected by the Pentagon. Yampol was also the national chair of the National Committee Against Nazi Criminals and Nazism in America, an organization that aggressively pursued Nazi war criminals.

He told the audience:

"We will never forget that tens of millions of people of all nationalities were killed or wounded in World War II. Hitler and the Nazis, who were responsible for that terrible war, brutally slaughtered civilians in the millions. Although some of the Nazi war criminals were punished after the Nuremberg trials, the world is shocked to learn, fifteen years after the war, that countless war criminals are still free and even hold top positions in the West German Government. Others live freely in England, Spain, Portugal, Austria, Egypt, France, Canada, various Latin American countries and in our own country. In most cases, they do so with the knowledge and protection of these governments. We share the growing concern of large numbers of Americans who are worried about the war criminals living in our country with the apparent approval of the U.S. State Department. Our committee hopes to work with any and all individuals and groups to bring about the extradition of these criminals so that they can stand trial in those countries where their crimes were committed.

"Failure to do so means that we are accomplices in shielding war criminals. More than that, it gives moral encouragement to native fascists of all types, including the Nazis who openly advocate a policy of genocide against Jews and Negroes"

The National Committee to Combat Nazism in 1963 held its convention in the city and was the subject of a Chicago Red Squad surveillance. Rabbi S. Burr Yampol was identified in the police department report as a "communist sympathizer."

It was at this convention, MJC President Milton Herst recalled, that two elderly women were allegedly hired by the Red Squad to release white mice into the Sherman Hotel banquet hall. The women were taken out of the room by police. A Chicago Police Department investigator's report confirmed the story. The meeting was disrupted by the release of white mice, but the women were not arrested.

On the occasion of the April 7, 1963 Warsaw Ghetto Uprising Commemoration, Aronin contributed what would be his final script, "The Guilty." It featured Cantor Moses Silverman, Everett Clarke, and his Art Theater Players. Erwin Jospe was at the piano.

Throughout the 1960s, Everett Clarke continued his dramatic presentations. Other famous actors who played various roles based on the Uprising joined him over the years. The list includes Luther Adler, Howard DaSilva, Nehamiah Persoff, and Israeli singer, Hanna Ahroni.

***

1964

The 21st Commemoration, was held April 9, 1964, at the Conrad Hilton Hotel. Speaking at the commemoration were Herman

Shumlin, the producer and director of *The Deputy,* and Polish Ambassador Edward Drozniak. Howard DaSilva performed the drama, "Warsaw Ghetto Uprising."

Chapter 13

The Mid-1960s:
A Renewed Commitment
to Civil Rights and Anti-Nazism

The MJC is "no hush, hush group," wrote Samuel L. Talmy in 1964. The Council's voice indeed was and would remain loud and clear. Speakers at commemorations in subsequent years would echo Ben Aronin's basic themes of fighting bigotry and resurrected Nazism by associating with the civil rights and anti-war movements.

MJC members were especially sensitive to the issues of civil rights. The commemorations had a two-fold purpose, the organization's leaders like to repeat: First, to keep the memory of the Martyrs sacred and alive. And second, the "commemorations must serve as a reminder to all people to stand on guard against the recurrence and resurgence of Nazism and the Hitler blueprint"

Because of their concerns, MJC organizers included leaders from the black and labor communities as speakers and planners for the commemorations. At a planning committee meeting in 1965, attorney Robert Feinglass reported on his participation in the civil rights voter registration drive in Mississippi.

***

1965

Speaking at the 22nd Commemoration on April 11, 1965, the Reverend Paul E. Turner, coordinator of the Mayor's Citizen Committee for a Better Chicago, connected Nazism with Racism in Selma, Alabama.

Reverend Turner said:

"From the past incidents concerning the death of
the three civil rights workers and the numerous racial
bombings in the South, it is evident that the hand of
the Nazi is still among us and now is the time to bring
an end to this work of the devil. We must not stand
idly by. It is the responsibility of every American to
support the Midwest Jewish Council in its fight to
extend the statute of limitations so that large numbers
of Nazi criminals will not go free."

By 1965, the candle lighters were all survivors. Saying
Kaddish for their own families as well as the other six million was
of double importance.

On June 13, 1965, MJC members mourned Samuel Talmy,
First Vice President and Chair of the Executive Board. Talmy, a
pharmacist, was born in Minsk, Russia. He came to the United States
in 1913, after escaping from the Russian army. A veteran of World
War I, he was a member of the American Legion and the Committee
Against Nazism as well as a supporter of most progressive causes,
movements and organizations. A memorial was inscribed for the
Reuven Brainin Clinic in Israel in Talmy's memory. His wife, Clara,
remained active with the MJC for many years.

***

1966

At the 23rd Commemoration April 9, 1966 at the Conrad
Hilton Hotel, Senator Wayne Morse (OR) spoke. After praising the
bravery of "the trapped Jews who resisted the well equipped Nazi
troops for six weeks" Morse called for support of the United Nations
and deplored the action of the U.S. State Department's support of
NATO. Political leaders were invited to speak.

Senator Morse addressed the commemorations in 1961, 1965 and 1966. Among the other popular politicians was Sen. Stephen M. Young of Ohio, who spoke for the years 1960 and 1963.

Also speaking at the 1966 Commemoration was the Reverend James Bevel of the West Side Christian Parish and Southern Christian Leadership Conference, who discussed the Jewish connection with the Civil Rights Movement.

Reverend Bevel compared the uprisings during the late 1960s in America's black Ghettos with the Warsaw Ghetto Uprising.

In 1966, Sidor Belarsky, a dramatic singer made his first of many appearances singing Jewish folk songs. Baruch Lumet, who was performing as the rabbi in "Fiddler on the Roof," recited poetry.

Equally important as the speakers and dramas at the commemorations were the resolutions on various social justice issues, which were endorsed at the commemorations.

In 1958, Philip Brail had presented a resolution for a Universal Memorial Day along with a resolution on Civil Rights. Among those presented during the 1960s were: A resolution on Genocide urging the U.S. Senate to ratify the United Nations Genocide Convention; a resolution on the American Nazi Party; a resolution on World Peace Disarmament and Nuclear Testing to End the Arms Race, and shift toward cooperative programs; and a resolution on the Middle East, which were addressed to the President and Congress.

***

1967

At the 24th Commemoration in the Conrad Hilton Hotel, Rabbi Abraham Feinberg of Toronto, Canada, spoke of his trip to Vietnam and conversing with North Vietnam leader Ho Chi Minh, a meeting that inspired hope for an end to the war. Such activities were, for certain, a red flag for the FBI. The MJC itself had been in the Red Squad files since the 1950s.

Chapter 14

1968
The 25ᵗʰ Commemoration

"It is most urgent that you attend this meeting and participate in these discussions." These words by Midwest Jewish Council President Herman Bush and Vice President Ann Laskin Hirsch followed an established annual pattern of urging people to help in the planning for the memorials.

With this request, they issued a call for the first brunch and planning meeting for the 25ᵗʰ Commemoration of the Warsaw Ghetto Uprising. It was held Sunday, September 17, 1967 at the Palmer House.

Following the planning brunch a series of planning activities proved a finely-tuned model of organizational efficiency and competence.

At a subsequent brunch in November, committees were appointed to prepare for a January conference when committee members were to report on progress for their plans. The committee decided to charge $1 for registration instead of the 50 cents admission that had been charged in the past.

Next came pre-commemoration conferences with featured speakers and other participants. At a luncheon meeting at the Conrad Hilton hotel in January 1968, Ann Hirsch introduced Ernest DeMaio, vice president and district president of the United Electrical Radio and Machine Workers of America, calling him a "fighter for peace." A week later, at the home of Mr. and Mrs. Israel Cutler, reports were made by program committees on the, program book and ticket sales. Other committees were created for ushers, and poster distribution.

The February brunch was called to discuss the 1968 Commemoration address a mailing list and install the officers. There were several pre-memorial conferences, which featured speakers as well as commemoration preparations.

During a March meeting the committee sent out 200 letters, each containing two tickets to various organizations and synagogues. The publicity and outreach announcements were prepared for newspapers, radio, and schools. Ann Hirsch pleaded:

> It is to those heroes of our days that we are paying tribute at the same time learning a lesson never to forget. I know we are all working hard so far, but this is not enough. The next few days are most important.

> We must sell tickets, contact people by phone and we must make sure that the Grand Ballroom will be filled to capacity. We have spared no efforts to arrange a very impressive program. You know as well as I do that numbers count.

April 21, 1968 arrived. The activists went to the Palmer House early to check on the arrangements. Two pennants, one in English, the other in Yiddish, were draped over the stage. Both declared the MJC theme: "Never to Forget and Never to Forgive."

Volunteers made certain that the platform for the dramatic presentation and the tables, each with candles, were properly arranged. Two fans were placed in such a way as to blow on both the American and Israeli flags as Phil Levinson sang the National Anthem and Hatikvah. Rabbi Menahim M. Goodman, of Congregation Anshe Motele, led the invocation. Ann Hirsch was chosen to make the opening remarks; she led a prayer for Herman Bush who was ill.

She then introduced the speakers sitting on the dais. Mrs. Hirsch described Alaska's Senator Ernest Gruening, the main speaker, as a "Humanitarian, a champion for world peace and a fighter for civil rights."

The senator spoke of an issue close to the hearts of this audience, Israel. Although Israel had been victorious during the six-day war of June 1967, American Jews had become aware that Israel's survival would lie with acceptance by the Arab world, not necessarily with the Europeans.

Senator Ernest Gruening called upon the assemblage to act as Americans, to support Israel against its Arab neighbors for the Arabs' purpose "is to destroy Israel."

Gerry Revzin retold the story of the Uprising in Yiddish, followed by actor Everett Clarke's narration of "The Eichmann Trial."

Cantor Louis Danto, himself a survivor and considered "one of the world's most famous cantors" came from the Park Synagogue of Cleveland Heights, Ohio, to sing songs of the Jewish people and the Ghetto. He chanted the El Mole Rachamim, as six women survivors kindled the Memorial Candles for the Six Million Martyrs. The Yahrzeit memorial candle lighters told stories that drew tears from the audience, a Chicago Tribune reporter wrote:

"My father picked me up and held me and ran away," said Ciporah Fox Katz. "I was lying under a pile of dead people. They thought I was dead."

"I crawled out of the Ghetto at night through a sewer," recalled Renny Kurshenbaum."

"They were chasing us, but we kept running. It was a miracle," remembered Sara Englander.

"We threw hot water on the Nazis when they came to kill us in the Ghetto, but they had tanks and guns and flame throwers" were the words of another survivor.

The 25th anniversary of the Warsaw Ghetto Uprising occurred in a particularly tumultuous year and the resolutions read by Phil Brail reflect these traumatic events. The meeting closed as all joined in the uplifting rendition of the Partisan Song.

Herman Bush, suffering from ill health, would be unable to attend any subsequent commemorations. While most letters and press releases continued to come from him as president, others now took on the bulk of the work.

Chapter 15

1969 to 1993
The Second 25 Years

The volunteers of the MJC who organized the commemorations followed the same successful format for the second 25 years that they had during the prior ones. They opened the evening with the singing of Hatikvah and the Star Spangled Banner, along with a rabbi's invocation. All events included the now traditional candle lighting ceremony for mourning, along with songs and dramatic readings to invoke and remember the past. The main speakers connected the past to the present. Always, the audience left the gathering uplifted by the message of survival from the collective singing of the Partisan Song.

During the second twenty five years, the meetings incorporated the phrases, "Remember the Kedoshim, holy martyrs of the Warsaw Ghetto," and then expanded the focus to commemorate the "Annihilation of our Six Million Martyrs and Millions of others."

***

1969

In 1969, attendance declined significantly. Many of the Jewish community moved to the suburbs. Such changes in socio-geographic patterns had their effects on events such as the commemorations.

The 26th Commemoration was held April 20th at the Sherman House.

Attendees heard Congressman Abner J. Mikva, who later served as a federal appeals court judge and White House Counsel, rally the audience, calling for a larger view in which the civil rights of all are espoused and protected.

The Adult Theatre of Henry Hart Jewish Community Center, staged "A Scene from the Wall," with Eddie Goldberg directing.

***

1970

Abraham Feinglass, vice president of the Amalgamated Meat Cutters & Butcher Workmen's Union (AMC & BWU) and president of the Fur and Leather Workers Union served as the main speaker for three years. Doing so first in 1970, he would return in that role in 1973 and 1979.

The commemoration was held April 12,1970, at the Sheridan Plaza Hotel.

***

1971

Hyde Park State Rep. Robert E. Mann, past president of the B'nai B'rith, was the main speaker at the 28th Commemoration April 25th. It was held at Northeastern Illinois State College.

Julius Schwarztein led the Chicago Jewish Peoples Choral Society in staging a dramatic presentation.

***

1972

At the LaSalle Hotel on April 16, 1972, Ann Hirsch welcomed the audience with the comments: "The Warsaw Ghetto Uprising and the Annihilation of our Six Million Martyrs now marks the 29th Yahrzeit sponsored by MJC under the leadership of our beloved President, Herman Bush, now deceased." She chaired the meetings along with Israel Cutler for a few more years, and later, Jack Altman became the co-chair.

***

1973

Robert Herbin, manager of the Chicago Joint Board of Fur, Leather and Luggage Workers Union, Chairman of the Trade Union Committee of Histadrut, and an officer of the Jewish Labor Committee, saved the day as speaker at the January planning conference. He also would serve as co-chair for the April 16 Commemoration.

With the help of organized labor, a tide had turned and a rising attendance sent the commemoration to Mather High School in Chicago from 1973 to 1980. The school auditorium seats 1,000 people. Earlier attitudes had faded away. Although the Jewish Labor Committee had originally refused to work with the MJC, by the 1970s, trade unionists had become active supporters. It then became just a question of time and of the rightness of the effort.

***

1974

Joseph Belsky, President of the AMC & BWU was scheduled as guest speaker in 1974. He, however, became ill four days before the event. Board member Zolman Emyanitoff, president of the Jewish Cultural Clubs of Chicago, substituted for him. The commemoration was held April 31 at Mather High School.

On the back of a "Dear Friends" request sent out for financial cooperation, 53 unions were listed, with each union indicating the number of tickets sold.

Chapter 16

The Continuing Challenge of Anti-Semitism

1975

The 32nd Commemoration was held April 20, 1975 and again at Mather High school.

Reaching out to minority groups, the committee had invited Charles Hayes, a prominent African-American union leader and a major player in several civil rights organizations, to be a speaker. Hayes served as vice president of the AMC & BWU, Illinois State AFL-CIO as well as president of the Chicago Chapter and vice president of the National Coalition of Black Trade Unionists.

Prominent civil rights attorney Irving G. Steinberg, who had defended many cases before the Supreme Court, also spoke. He recounted the "diabolically clever" Nazi plan "to use Jews against Jews to liquidate the Warsaw Ghetto." Steinberg urged cooperation with trade unions and the "legal outlawing of all racist, chauvinist expressions and action." He urged the "ratification of the Genocide Convention, and the comprehensive exposure of discrimination in employment and housing."

Soprano Rose Fogelman, with Esther Levinson on the piano, as part of the program offered a dramatic presentation of "Faith in Our People."

***

1976

The 33rd Commemoration was held April 11, 1976 at Mather High School. Irving Steinberg was again the main speaker. The civil rights lawyer reiterated the time-worn anti-Semitic cliches made by American political leaders over the years, always reminding his audience that anti-Semitism never rests. He discovered "the rise of the ultra-right conservative movements" in West Germany where "there is a growing wave of nostalgia for Hitler's cowlick and for Goering's uniforms." He spoke of Canada, where a pamphlet was being widely circulated entitled, "Did six million die—the truth at last?"

Steinberg reminded listeners of the desecration of synagogues and cemeteries in Milwaukee, Aurora and Cicero. The lawyer also recited lies being spread by the American Nazi Party, the John Birch Society, the Liberty Lobby, and the National State-Rights Party.

He added, "In the 1920s, Nazis were ignored. Nazi votes were considered small. Are we in the same position in the United States today?" he wondered. Steinberg effectively dismissed Black anti-Semitism as a fraud leading "into a blind alley. The hour calls for building Jewish/Black unity as well as unity with the Chicano, Puerto Rican and other oppressed people."

The Jewish Community Center of Milwaukee Players presented "The Diary of Anne Frank."

***

1977

At the 34th Commemoration April 17, 1977, held at Mather High school, Northwestern University Professor Irwin Weil spoke. He was chairman of the Slavic Language Department there.

A student, Jeffrey Sanders read poetry.

***

1978

The 35th Commemoration was held April 16, 1978 at Mather High School. The danger of the resurgence of Nazism had been woven into the threads of the commemorations over prior years by civil rights attorney Irving Steinberg. He was again the principal speaker at the 1978 Commemoration.

By this time, Steinberg was anything but complacent about the Skokie case. He perceived the Nazi march in the U.S. the same as occurred in Germany. No one would ever consider him anything but outspoken; he always called things the way he saw them. Steinberg challenged, "How can the Nazis and the Ku Klux Klan operate openly, with arsenals? What other group has gotten the kind of media attention given the Klan?"

According to his wife Judy, Steinberg had come up from the Depression years with the experiences that molded him into a staunch progressive. He chose his clients carefully, filtering out those "richer folks" whom he believed were able to afford a higher priced attorney.

"He worked," Judy said, "for those who needed assistance, who needed justice, and he made a point of that. He had a passion for social justice, and worked tirelessly for those who just did not get proper representation in the courts. This included a commitment to minorities, to the poor, or anyone who was not getting a fair chance."

"He always told his clients," she continued, "'You'll pay me when you can.' He never stopped fighting the establishment."

A drama was presented as part of the commemoration program by Paul Barnes and Dorothy Jordan.

***

1979

Abraham Feinglass, vice president of the AMC & BWU and president of the Fur and Leather Workers Union, again was the main speaker. The commemoration was held April 22 at Mather High School

Music was provided by flutist Joan Bowman with Sonia Kass accompanying her on the piano.

Chapter 17

The Nazis March on Skokie and Other Issues

In 1977, a group of Nazis, frustrated by confrontations with angry protesters in Chicago's Marquette Park, sent applications for demonstration permits to North Shore suburbs. Only Skokie, a community with a very large Jewish Holocaust survivor population, responded. As a result, the idea that Nazis would be given permission to march down the streets of this peaceful, law-abiding suburb created a response that was both emotional and loud.

National media picked up the story of this possible event, which was supported by the ACLU, despite deep internal divisions within that civil liberties group. Many members resigned from the ACLU over the issue, while others deliberately took out memberships.

The issues were complex and reached deeply into the sense of justice on both sides. Soon, national eyes were on the Skokie struggle. Emotional responses to the Nazi threat stirred many Jews and non-Jews to both sides of the cause.

Some had been ardent civil libertarians and had taken the stand that in order to preserve the civil liberties of all, it was necessary to allow the Nazis to march down the streets of Skokie however hateful would be their presence. Others, especially the survivors, were aghast at the idea that people who had done everything in their power to destroy the civil liberties of millions would now be allowed to publicly demonstrate with their hateful symbols on the streets of their town.

While the National Socialist Party threatened to march in Skokie between December 1976 and June 1978 in fact, they never did. Memories of this conflict, however, remain powerful in the minds of many. Skokie is the home of the Illinois Holocaust Memorial Foundation. In addition, Skokie was selected as the site for a Holocaust memorial by the Chicago Area Holocaust Survivors organization. A bronze sculpture depicting a freedom fighter, a mother mourning her slain child and a rabbi comforting a little boy was built in 1987 with support from MJC.

Erna Gans, president of the Holocaust Memorial Foundation until her death in 1999, had been an active participant in the Skokie conflict and in the survivors organization, and had been chosen as one of the candle lighters between 1981-1984. She and Judy Lachman, a survivor and another active participant in the Holocaust Memorial Foundation of Illinois, were at MJC planning meetings and had been involved in reporting on the progress of the Museum and the Holocaust Library, which is now part of the Foundation.

Chapter 18

Accomplishments Despite Diminished Energy and Support

1980

The 37th Commemoration was held April 27, 1980 at Mather High School. "Former Nazis living in the United States" was the topic in 1980 when Charles Nicodemus, *Chicago Sun-Times* reporter gave the keynote address. Nicodemus had distinguished himself with awards for a variety of stories, including a series investigating war crimes suspects Frank Walus and Liudas Kairys in Chicago and John Demjanjuk in Cleveland. His work and his concerns endeared him to the audience.

Gil Parker read the work, "Poems of the Ghetto"

***

1981

By 1981, the audience had slimmed down and the committee was forced to search out a smaller auditorium. They were then welcomed by Dr. F. Burton Nelson, professor of theology at North Park College and an expert on the Holocaust. Civil rights attorney Irving G. Steinberg was again the speaker as was Esther Fink of the Association of Children of Survivors. The dramatic presentation was a Byrne Piven Theater Workshop version of "A Little Lower than the Angels."

It included the following:

Graffiti on a concentration camp wall:
'I believe in the sun even if it is not shining.
'I believe in man even when I am alone.
'I believe in God even when he is silent.'
"By remembering we mean to turn to the light in the wholeness of our humanity.

"Rabbi Yehudi said: 'Our mission is not to be realms in which dwell the purity of holiness; it is to the unholy that we must pay attention so that it find redemption and become whole.'

"Never shall I forget that night, the first night in camp which has turned my life into one long night;

"Never shall I forget the little faces of the children, whose bodies I saw turned into wreaths of smoke beneath a silent blue sky.

"Never shall I forget that nocturnal silence which deprived me, for all eternity, of the desire to live.

"Never shall I forget those moments which murdered my God and my soul and turned my dreams to dust.

"Never shall I forget these things, even if I am condemned to live as long as God himself. Never.

"At Auschwitz, tell me, where was God? Answer: Where was Man?"

***

1982

In 1982, at the 39th Commemoration at North Park College the future mayor of Chicago,Congressman Harold Washington was the guest speaker. He had served sixteen outstanding years in the state legislature.In he U.S.Congress, he was on the Judiciary,Education, Labor and Government Opertion committees.He was also secretary of the Congressional Black Caucus and a life-long activist for civil rights, affirmative action and equal employment opportunity.

The Congressman opened his remarks with:

Kain mol nish fargessen (Never to forget). It serves no useful purpose for any of us to compare our fight. Suffice to say the genocidal pattern perpetuated against Black people in this world for years is unique in terms of history with such intensive degree of hatred that amazes you.

I served in the army during World War II and I struggled to try to understand what forced people to do such evil. This country was not pure during those times. It did not open its doors to Jewish refugees from Nazi persecution.

I marched in Marquette Park with Rabbi Robert Marx. I cannot separate the plight of the Jewish people; the pattern of anti-Semitism and anti-Black racism is inseparable. One does not forget the rise of the KKK, Nazi activities, White Citizen Councils and even the moral majority.

It's crazy, we have too many nuclear weapons; they are taking away our civil liberties; cutting the budget for legal services, education and voting rights. Your resolutions on civil rights, against war, on genocide are right on target.

We stand here strong. We will fight back and not permit them to throw us back into the morass. I will close *"Kain mol nish fargessen."*

The dramatic presentation by Am Chai was titled "Resistance in the Bialystock Ghetto."

***

1983

In 1983, an election of officers was held several months before the 40th Commemoration. Ann Hirsch,at the age of 86was compelled to taper off her activities.Her life (1895-1991) was long and active.Because of her age,she moved into the role of President Emeritus,Milton Herst,co-chair the previous year,was elected president

Concern for Israel, was always a major topic at the commemorations. The 40th Commemoration was held at Mather High school on April 17, 1983. Avri Fischer, Commander of a Medical unit during the Yom Kippur War, was the guest speaker. A member of the Kibbutz Artzi Federation of Kibbutzim, he was also head of the Hashomer Hatzair World Movement, the party of Mordechai Anielewicz, leader of the Warsaw Ghetto Uprising.

***

1984

The 41st Commemoration was held April 8 at North Park College.

Guest speaker Charles Allen, a Quaker and author of *Nazi War Criminals Among Us,* connected U.S. policy of granting asylum to Nazi war criminals to the Cold War. As an internationally published author, journalist, editor and lecturer, Allen was considered America's pre-eminent authority on Nazi war criminals living in the United States.

In 1978, he testified as an expert witness on Nazi war criminals before the Judiciary Committee of the U.S. House of Representatives. His writings, concerned primarily with racism, anti-Semitism and fascism, have been called 'brilliant' and 'powerful' by nine Nobel Prize Laureates.

Allen reminded the listeners of "these Nazi criminals living among us, freely since 1945. Some of them were used by the U.S. government in the name of 'fighting communism,' a rationale of Hitler and fascism. These Nazis were being used by the counter intelligence corps of the United States Army immediately after the war."

Allen also mentioned Pope Pius XII silence of complicity based on newly discovered revelations. The Vatican immediately after WW II, had established escape routes that helped people like Klaus Barbie, Eichmann and other Nazi war criminals escape.

Warning of the dangers of a nuclear holocaust, Allen then stated,

Our obligation is to learn by examining the historical records. The Warsaw Ghetto Uprising was not a struggle for defense of a piece of earth; not a struggle to save lives of dear ones, because most were already murdered; not a struggle to save one's own life, because one's own life was difficult to endure in any case. It was a struggle generated by a driving moral purpose on a much higher plane. This was a struggle for a people, for its future, a determination to uphold the honor of the Jewish people.

The Jews of Warsaw upheld the honor and dignity of mankind itself. There is no difference whatsoever between the use of former Nazi terrorists of the Holocaust period and the terrorists systematically used in Vietnam, Iran, Chile, South Africa, Central America, Nicaragua and elsewhere. We must heed the lesson, so that the final nuclear holocaust, will not happen.

In quoting from Emil Fackanheim, philosopher and Auschwitz survivor, Allen stated, "that a Jew is forbidden to give Hitler a posthumous victory.' I can only add that the obligation is to all peoples, non-Jews as well. There must never be a second Holocaust."

Allen went on to identify with the present day struggles of "all of us, Jew and non-Jew, white, black, and all peoples struggling against oppression, struggling just to live a life of dignity."

The Florence Heller Jewish Community Center ensemble presented the Uri Suhl drama "They Fought Back." It was directed by Linda Sherman.

***

1985

The guest speaker at 42nd Commemoration ,April 21,1985 at North Park College was Erwin (Bud) Salk author, lecturer, businessman and history instructor at Columbia College. He was past president of B'nai B'rith, Past Vice-President of the Jewish Council on Urban Affairs, founder and organizer of Businessmen Move for Vietnam Peace, and delegate to the World Peace Conference in Sofia, Bulgaria.

He told the audience:

Today is a momentous occasion, never forgetting the history of the Warsaw Ghetto Uprising. We must examine the meaning of the Holocaust and insure that there never will be another Holocaust anywhere again.

How do we explain, despite hundreds of speeches, articles, and books written about the Holocaust that most Jews have no idea what actually brought it about? More importantly why do they fail to grasp its obvious lesson?

This was a ruthless dictatorship of the most reactionary elements of finance capital. Fascism lives when they are no longer able to control the people through democratic means.

My basic thesis today is very simple: there is no more important subject than U.S.and USSR relations. We in the business community made an amazing discovery--that these nuclear bombs and weapons do not discriminate between communist or capitalist or Jew and gentile or black and white men, women and children.

I just returned from Washington, DC, where I spent a day with Carl Sagan who gave an excellent talk on Nuclear Winter. This concept puts a deep shade on how bad the Holocaust was.

I teach about the missing pages in U.S. history at Columbia College. It could expand to World History when dealing with the Holocaust. It's imperative we include the

fact twelve million people were exterminated by the Nazis. This includes six million Jews, gypsies, homosexuals, and Poles as well as twenty million Russians.

The Nazis destroyed seventeen hundred Soviet cities, more than seventy thousand Soviet villages, thirty two thousand industrial enterprises and left nearly twenty five million homeless Russians.

David Weiman wrote *The Abandonment of the Jews: America and the Holocaust.* The book describes the role the United States and Great Britain played in not taking in Jews, not even up to the quotas, and doing nothing because of the virulent anti-Semitism that existed in the United States. The USSR saved thousands of Jews from Poland and other parts of Europe.

Unfortunately our government has had the policy since World War I and II—as described by Walter Lippman, of wishing to destroy the Soviet Union. The danger exists in bringing about a nuclear winter unless we find a policy of détente.

The embargo against the USSR costs our economy over forty billion dollars, and crippled many agribusinesses. These contracts are going to Western Europe, Japan, and other parts of the world. We should place our emphasis on trade, cultural and scientific exchanges and athletic competition.

Right now there are six Tennessee Williams plays showing in Moscow. We are going to live together or die together.

Robert Skeist, a board member and active with "Chicago Friends of Peace Now", also spoke and discussed the Middle East Peace process.

Byrne and Joyce Piven again presented "A Little Lower Than the Angels."

***

1986

The 43rd Commemoration was held April 13, again at North Park College. The guest speaker was the owner and editor of *The Sentinel,* Jack Fishbein. He had long been a Jewish activist and force for unity of Jews in Chicago. In his speech he renewed his earlier message with a summons "to clean away the chometz," food that is not kosher for Passover.

He proclaimed: "We have only two choices... Either we learn to live with the Soviets, though we disagree with their philosophy or we go to war with them. I prefer the former."

Fishbein scolded both right wing and leftist Jewish journalists. "But the spirit of those Ghetto fighters give me strength and I hope they will also give those of you who hesitate, new strength to carry on the struggle to save the world from nuclear destruction."

Mayor Harold Washington, presented greetings from the City of Chicago, and praised Fishbein as "a modern day Don Quixote," serving as, "an historic bond between Black Americans and the Jewish People."

Dina Halpern performed in a dramatic presentation.

At the same program, George Landman (1909-1995) reinforced this connection in his Yiddish speech:

I am a working man, not a public speaker. I am the survivor of a large family. They and 400 other families were murdered on August 1, 1941, when the Nazis came to Telachan, Byelorussia, my hometown. Their only sin was that they were Jewish.

Now when we memorialize those who died in Warsaw and other ghettos, we are faced with a new danger. Anti-Semitism is on the rise. Neo-Nazi organizations are multiplying. Other right-wing organizations are advocating violent actions against Jews, Blacks, Latinos and other peoples. We must fight all manifestations of anti-Semitism and racism.

George Landman, in English, concluded his remarks celebrating another goal close to his heart:

We are happy to see the active participation of so many young people in today's program. We of the Midwest Jewish Council call on our children and grandchildren to share our work.

Landman was a leader in the International Ladies Garment Workers Union and the Jewish Labor Committee. He was MJC ticket chairperson and treasurer from 1976 until his death in 1995.

Six women survivors passed on their legacy to their children and grandchildren who then were given the honor to light the candles. When George Landman translated into Yiddish a ceremony first used by an international gathering of survivors in Jerusalem, the rendition was simultaneously read in English by six survivors.

Then six children of survivors walked onto the stage, each carrying a candle and responded:

"We accept the obligation of this legacy, to remember, to tell the world, to fight anti-Semitism and all forms of racial hatred, to remember the miracle of the Jewish rebirth in the land of our ancestors in Israel."

Cantor Pavel Slavensky chanted the El Mole Rachaminm, and the Partisan Song.

The programs were always designed to accomplish several goals: they were to remind those present never to forget and they were focused on addressing those political and social issues that were of pressing import to the Jewish community at the time. Thus, in addition to dramatic and musical performances--which always engrossed the audiences, speeches were given by outstanding leaders within the community.

***

1987

MJC's concern for contemporary social justice issues continued with the group's advocacy of health care reform.

The 44th Commemoration was held April 26, 1987 at North Park College. The guest speaker was Ruth Rothstein, then president and chief executive officer at Mount Sinai Medical Center and the Schwab Rehabilitation Center.

Always visionary, Rothstein went on to become head of Cook County Hospital. Over a lifetime, she has received countless awards for her civic, labor and social activities, including a honorary Doctor of Law degree from Kenyon College in Ohio, and Doctor of Humane Letters, Rush University College, Chicago, and a special award from *Ms.* Magazine. She was joined at the podium by the Reverend Hycel Taylor pastor of the Second Baptist Church of Evanston and past professor at Garrett Evangelical Theological Seminary.

Reverend Taylor reminded the audience that he was representing his people and his church, and was, as a black man, there "to join with you who have suffered." He spoke of what it means to be African-American, making clear he understood the importance for Jews to have Israel. He himself had been to Israel, seen the Yad Vashem and had also been to West Africa where he observed many similarities in cruelty.

"I empathize with suffering," he said. "We know you have been there. Hitler's personality still lives. We see cruelty still, we see our own people, and we see Hispanic and Latino people incarcerated. We've been through the fires of hell. We see the earth's resources shrinking. We can no longer fight one another. There must be no more fighting, no more killing. We must rise above hatred, injustice everywhere. We must insure that the Holocaust never, never, never happens again."

It was a rousing speech, and the audience responded enthusiastically.

When Ruth Rothstein followed, her presentation became the ultimate rationale, the shining and eloquent reasons why MJC had to continue its fight for the good.

She told the audience:

The Holocaust has meaning for me, and for all Jews. It gives us all a greater purpose, a mandate to seek justice and goodness for all our days. As Jews, we are bound to follow moral and ethical principles for a just society. We must be eternally vigilant. Even our own Jewish traditions mandate that we must not just protect Jews, we must protect all men.

These lessons are part of my history. I was taught warmth, compassion, and social consciousness. As a young child, I was taken by my parents to rallies where we learned about Germany and the war.

I knew it was true, although there were deniers who said it couldn't be so. Millions perished. And I've taught my own children it must never happen again to any peoples.

We must continue. We must protect the principles of social justice, ethics and morality. We must protect free speech for all. As Jews and as Americans, we must show respect for the individual, concern for civil rights, foster an educated electorate, work for social justice. We must protect these principles. And we must be optimistic.

We must believe we can make the world better. We must find the joys in our lives. We must believe in the wholesome pursuit of a good life. But we also must believe in acts of charity and acts of justice. As for charity, Jews unstintingly give to our own; and they unstintingly give to non-Jews as well. As for justice, we must ensure society will not restrict the individual.

Jews must also be of service. Jews died in Mississippi in the support of civil rights. It takes guts to speak out. Silence ensures another Hitler. In the pursuit of justice, Jews have no choice but to be strong in both words and deeds.

Rothstein then went on to describe the Warsaw Ghetto Uprising and the several hundred who were poorly armed, poorly equipped, and yet who fought with valor.

Each fighter knew it was an unequal fight; yet they fought making my own dreams of how valor can become true. They were slaves, yet they resisted; they fought back, every day a new challenge to those who risked their lives. The pain, the memories of the camps all this sensitizes us to the injustice of all peoples.

Every day we must speak out for freedom and justice against hatred and oppression. We must use our strength to make a moral light for the future. Apartheid, racism, anti-Semitism it's all the same, and we cannot afford to tolerate any form of racism.

We must also speak out on behalf of women, who are the most impoverished group in the country. We must speak out against evil, even our own evil as Jews, whether it be on the battlefield or on Wall Street. It's a "shanda" (shame) when well-known Jews turn their energies into raw greed. (She then mentioned the names of the most prominent Jewish traders who were sentenced to jail for their underhanded financial dealings.)

we must speak out even when Israel is wrong. While Jews must support Israel, we must also speak out when we see wrongs done there as well. We must express outrage wherever it exists.

Action is not a spectator ideology. "There are joys in being Jewish," she affirmed. "But, I will say firmly, 'We will never forget. We will never forgive.'"

Chicago Symphony Orchestra cellist Roberta Guastafeste Performed during the Candle Lighting Ceremony

Chapter 19

The Final Years:
The Course Is Stayed

1988

The 45th Commemoration of the Warsaw Ghetto Uprising was held April 17 at Mather High School. The guest speaker was attorney and long-time Chicago alderman of the 5th Ward, Leon (Len) M. Despres. Respected as the conscience of the City Council, and perceived as a single-handed counter-balance to Chicago's first Mayor Richard J. Daley and clout, he had been re-elected four times.

This aggressive advocate for civil liberties and justice had been a vigorous fighter for years, having been general counsel for the American Civil Liberties Union (1948-1955), and an academic. He taught courses in labor law and collective bargaining at the University of Chicago Law School, Roosevelt University, and the University of Wisconsin. He also has authored several law review articles.

His honors and awards are many while his civic activities would fill many pages on any resume. And his passion for justice has never wavered.

The words of Leon Despres were exhilarating and inspiring:

Today, we must celebrate the unshakeable human spirit of man. What do these Warsaw warriors tell us? They tell us to remember. We need to repeat the story of their deeds, we need to tell the story to our children. We can't repeat it too often. Then the former alderman quoted the numbers for the Ghetto:

In July 1942, there were 350,000 in the Warsaw Ghetto. It was hell on earth. By September 1942, all the Jews were told to move to a tiny, restricted area. A number had become suspicious of the lies, of the promises of work elsewhere, of the postcards sent back to them telling them how good it was.

In response, the Ghetto dwellers sent an Aryan-looking Jew out into the larger world, and he came back with the truth. He told them of the camps where no Jew survived.

By Yom Kippur, 1942, there were less than 45,000 in the Ghetto, with 10,000 a day being deported. Even deported were the 2,000 Jewish policemen, who had been given special privileges to do their dirty work. They were now considered expendable and were deported.

By September 20, there was a call to action. The leadership organized, and the word went out. 'We will die with honor' became the cry. And the call went out to raise money for arms, ammunition, to gather all possible resources for a response.

On January 18, 1943, German troops came into the Ghetto and Jewish fighters killed 50 of them. The act electrified the Ghetto. People went underground, found ways to survive and plan. Telegrams were sent out to the Polish government in exile and to the United States.

The appeals went unanswered.

By April 19, 1943, 2,000 Germans entered the Ghetto. And the Uprising began. Two hundred were killed and the Germans had retreated.

By May 10, the Germans covered up all exits and used poison gas; a mere 43 the last stronghold survived. And 75 had escaped.

The Ghetto was totally destroyed. Six centuries of culture and history came to an end. The history of Einstein, Freud, poets, artists and scientists. It all came to an end.

For each survivor we are grateful. They tell us to remember. Evil does exist; but, history tells us, we can keep it at bay--we can do it. The odds may be hopeless, but we must combat it.

Our history tells us we can and have. Look at the Pharaohs and the Exodus, the Macabees' fight in Syria, the Continental Congress that fought back the entire British Navy, the Masada. Resistance is the word. It sets the standards for us; it enables us to carry on.

And today, we can turn no deaf ear where there is need: South Africa, the B'hai, the refuseniks, the fighters in Nicaragua.

We are here to honor resistance to evil across the globe, and in our own U.S. history. We honor the slaves, Sojourner Truth, Frederick Douglass and the Indians. We are for LIFE. We must never lose such commitment. The Jews have been slaves, exiles, persecuted, tortured, and besieged. We understand suffering and injustice. We are not to be passive. We do not turn our backs to others.

Indeed, Len Despres spoke for the entire MJC membership, which had long understood that suffering was not unique to the Jews.

In 1988, a number of other outstanding Jewish leaders participated.

Heather Booth, president of Citizen Action and the Midwest Academy—the nation's largest grassroots progressive organization—was committed to wining economic democracy and social justice for all people.

The Midwest Academy offered a training center for social activists who found their efforts ennobled by the creative methods employed to effect social change. One and a half million members belong to the Midwest Academy across the country and Booth has played a significant role in the Academy's success. Her own career worked closely with the progressive branch of the Democratic Party in Washington, D.C., with her leadership skills much sought after. Booth, before the candle lighting ceremony, said:

> Every generation must tell anew the story of the Holocaust and the story of the ways all of us are survivors, all our families are survivors. Our feelings are deep, our commitments are equally deep. We must never let any injustice to any people go by without commitment to that struggle. We light candles for a vision for the hope of the future. These are candles against the darkness.

Also on the dias was Reverend Kenneth Smith, a leader and visionary who had over a long career, showed a unique level of courage and commitment to human rights for all the people in the city. Dr. Smith was then president of and associate professor at the Chicago Theological Seminary, minister of the United Church of Christ and on the board of directors of the National Conference of Christians and Jews. He was former president of the Community Renewal Society and past president of the Chicago Board of Education. He spoke these words:

> The world has never treated dreamers favorably and with kindness. The world tends to destroy dreamers. The world has not been able to destroy the dreams centuries after centuries, dreams which are incorporated into the lives of successive generations of people. We must be more than dreamers; we must be doers as well.

> We dream of a world without anti-Semitism, or racism, or Nazism. We know they are anti-human and destructive to the human spirit. Therefore we must commit ourselves anew to these ends so that our children and our children's children will stand tall against the carriers of such thinking. We must work to make certain that institutional and structural anti-Semitism and Nazism and racism are eradicated from our world. We must work as a mighty moral army.

We understand and we want the world to understand that each man, woman and child are individual gifts.

As such, not one hair upon their heads should ever be harmed. Let us as a chorus drown out the negative voices, the subtle suggestions of evil, which we decry and deplore. Let us walk together and never grow weary in the long pilgrimage of this life.

We are the bearers of light in place of darkness and may our flames never go out so together we can say, "never again to slavery and never again to the Holocaust."

Actor Jerry Jarret then read a moving dramatic presentation, "And the Earth Rebelled" by Yuri Suhl.

***

1989

The 46th Commemoration was held April 16, 1989 at Mather High School. Sondra Gair, known for her news-breaking stories of world affairs which were broadcast on Chicago National Public Radio station, WBEZ, was guest speaker.

She had developed a reputation for cutting-edge stories that no other mainstream station would touch; her coverage of the issues around the Iran-Contra Affair became essential listening for most Chicagoans concerned with our country's complicity in illegally bringing drugs to the U.S. in exchange for illegally supporting the Contras during the Nicaraguan civil war.

***

1990

The 47th Commemoration was held April 29, 1990 at Mather High School.

Dr. Quentin Young, long-time healthcare reform advocate. Dr. Young—who became a regular medical talk show host on National Public Radio affiliate, WBEZ—is the founder of the Health and Medicine Policy Research Group, an advocacy group identifying public health trends in the U.S. The doctor is well known in the Chicago area as a progressive voice for medical reform and for single-payer health insurance

Dr. Young, now in his 80s, still practices medicine and is affiliated with University of Chicago Hospitals and Michael Reese Hospital..

He spoke eloquently:

> The cruelest forces that society created were created by Hitler. How close the world came to fall under the heel of the Nazi brutes and how close the final disaster came just within months. It took tremendous strength of all the powers of the East and West to finally overcome that monstrosity.
>
> We understood after Spain, after the conquest of Europe, after Pearl Harbor, after the Holocaust, how grim the future looked. We live in fear of the return of Fascist domination. Now we have the awesome fear of equal magnitude of the ever presence of a nuclear holocaust that has the power to destroy the world.
>
> Our human condition is a vicious predatory, murderous, raping, stealing spectacle. Ninety-nine percent in recorded history gives witness to that. Only one percent shows that we have a courageous, altruistic, unselfish, sacrificing side, and we live by those values that inspires us. Unless that side becomes dominant we will lose not only our lives, the lives of our children, but the world.
>
> Fortunately, we won in the last part of the Century.

***

1991

On April 14, 1991 at the 48th Commemoration at Mather High School, a distinguished panel focused on "The Impact of the Holocaust on the Jews of Tomorrow." Rabbi Philip Lefkowitz, chairman of the Political Action Committee of the Chicago Rabbinical Council and a leading member of the Religious Zionists of the Midwest, discussed, "Diaspora Jews and their Relationship with Israel."

In 1991, Israel was exploring peace with Palestinians in Madrid, the precursor to the Oslo agreements. Rabbi Lefkowitz, emphasizing the importance of the return to the Jewish homeland and kinship between all Jews to the little state, criticized American Jews:

> The view of creating an Israel for the unfortunate Jew, not for the Jewish people, not for every Jewish soul, but those in pain and those in suffering became the cornerstone of American Jewish feelings toward the Jewish state. We can take on the Palestinians, take on its hostile neighbors, and even the wavering and meandering of American policy.
>
> But the turning away from the State of Israel by the Jewish community in America cannot be endured. We must remember that Israel is not just another country, not even just another democracy, but it is the very fiber and rock of our soul, holy and sacred to every one of us. We all bemoan the fact that the Holocaust, in many ways, was a result of the fact that there was no State of Israel. We joyfully and willingly accept a miracle today in the exodus of millions of Jews being saved because there is a land of Israel. It must be defended with our every breath and souls.

Let us pray for peace in the Middle East, peace for Arab, peace for Israel, peace for Jew, Christian and Muslim. May that peace radiate to the four corners of the earth and bring peace, wealth and joy to all humanity.

When the founder of the Jewish Council on Urban Affairs, Rabbi Robert Marx, of Congregation Hakafa came to talk, his topic, "Causes and effects of anti-Semitism and Racism," was a subject that the Rabbi had contemplated for a number of years.

He coupled his remarks with Eli Weisel's question. "How could the Jewish community stand there while the body of a young man was hung? How could they stand there silently?" Somehow, the rabbi believes that some Jewish actions of "separation," of segregating one group from another, of making one group "less" than the other plays a vital role in societal injustice. His words included:

The first thing we must examine is how separations occur in society. The first act of the Nazi was to separate the Jews. Jewish stores were closed and the Yellow Star of David had to be worn on outer garments. The idea of separation is both beautiful and painful. Ideas of Jewish and Christian history abound with climbing up and down, Moses was given the Torah at Mt. Sinai; Isaiah pictures the end of days at the top of the mountain. Jesus' sermon is given on the Mount. Over and over again, the idea of rising is important.

One elevates himself in Western thought rather than debases himself. This debasement has created tragedy because when there is up and down, there is a lofty people, Germans; and a base people, Jews.

The second complication comes when power is added to the idea of 'up and down.' They create a separation, which can be disastrous. In the Ghetto, in the Pale of Settlement, the lower were separated from the high because they were unworthy, because they have disabilities, because they were considered base and sick and evil.

In Europe as well as here in this country, a people were separated from the other people made low. In the concentration camps of Europe, Jews were made to feel that they were unworthy, that they were low. Disabilities were heaped upon disabilities, until destruction followed.

The third element of anti-Semitism is indifference. Concentration of Jews was the only time in recorded history where people were consciously segregated for purpose of extermination. Indifference affects our response to the Kurds of Northern Iraq, who are experiencing their great catastrophe today as are people in the inner cities deprived of health care, those who are neglected.

Those in my congregation say they are so far away, what can we do? But weren't those exactly the words said of Jews in the concentration camps of Auschwitz in 1943?

We must all respond we must fight indifference, we must hear, we must bring down the lofty when they gain a power that becomes oppressive to the poor, the lowly, the sick, the wounded, the helpless. We can act, we must go, we must listen and we must do.

The third speaker was Gerry Revzin, executive director of the Congress of Secular Jewish Organizations of North America and vice chair of the International Federation of Secular Humanistic Jews. She had been a regular participant in the commemorations and her focus was "Teaching the Lessons of the Holocaust."

She began her speech with the question, "What legacy do we want to leave to our children, grandchildren, and future generations to come?"

Dismissing those who say it's time to forget, Revzin cited the Spanish philosopher, Santayana, "Those who refuse to study and learn from history are doomed to relive it."

Revzin quoted several studies indicating "That anti-Semitism and pro-Nazi feelings still exist and persist" in Europe, the USSR, Japan and the United States. In Austria, a program encourages survivors to visit the schools to relate their experiences became part of the curriculum in the 1980s.

Revzin described a museum in Melbourne, Australia, which was established by survivors of the Lodz Ghetto. The Melbourne Ministry of Education included mandatory visits to the museum for the course of study in their public high schools.

***

1992

In August 1991, Honorable Philip M. Klutznick, past president of the World Jewish Congress and former U.S. Secretary of Commerce, had agreed to honor the organization as our guest speaker at the 49th Commemoration on April 12, 1992.

On January 19, 1992, however, the Midwest Jewish Council was informed that Mr. Klutznick's ill health would regrettably not allow him to participate at the commemoration

Alderman Lawrence Bloom from Chicago's 5th Ward substituted as guest speaker. Ald. Bloom was principal of the South Side School of Jewish Studies and vice president of K.A.M. Isaiah Israel Congregation.

On the same program, Marilyn Price, nationally-known puppeteer and storyteller offered the following apt fable:

Something is happening here. There is a man
with a gun over there. You better stop children, look
around something is coming down.

It was peaceful in the forest. The birds flitted and flew, the porcupines walked along with spiny quills, laid back, quiet. The squirrels chattered with their bushy tails. The frogs hopped, the fish swam with their scales glistening in the sun. The little rabbit with his father smiled as a rabbit could smile.

"Oh it's peaceful in the forest," said the rabbit. "Yes my son, all is peaceful."

Until the day the terrible things came. The shadow covered the forest and the noise was terrible and so were the smells. They quickly covered the forest with their nets and said, 'We want all things with feathers.' The birds looked quickly for a place to hide; they flittered. They flew as fast as they could but the nets caught them and dragged them away.

And it was quiet in the forest. The little rabbit said to his father, "Why did they take away the birds?" And the rabbit said, "It makes no difference. You don't have feathers, pay no attention." So all was peaceful in the forest. Oh yes, there were no birds but there were porcupines. Oh, the squirrels with their bushy tails they climbed the trees, they chattered as squirrels do in the spring. In the summer all was peaceful and the water shone on the fishes back.

And then they came again with their terrible smell, their terrible noises. "We want all things with bushy tails." Quickly the rabbit turned around. "We don't have bushy tails, just short little tails--not us, don't take us," and they didn't.

Oh, the squirrels scurried away. They chattered, they raced as fast as they could but the nets flew out and the squirrels were taken. The little rabbit said to his father, "Why do they want bushy tails and feathers?" It doesn't matter; they make too much noise anyway and those squirrels were fussy and they were stealing things that belong to us. It doesn't matter. Mind your own business," and he did.

And it was peaceful in the forest. Oh yes the frogs hopped and the fish swam and the sun caught on their scaly backs. It was beautiful, quieter than before and all things were peaceful, until they came again with their terrible noises and their terrible smells and their terrible roars. Quickly they said, "We want all things that swim in the water." The fish tried to escape, they really did. They jumped out of the water. They could have flown if only their wishes came true but they didn't. The terrible things with their terrible nets swooped down through the water and dragged away the fish and frogs and all that lived underneath and they were gone.

And the little rabbit turned to his father. "Why did they want the fish? Why did they want the squirrels with bushy tails? Why did they want the birds that fluttered?" And his father said, "Never mind, keep out of sight." And so they did. Yet, for the next time there came the terrible smell and terrible noises. They wanted all things with spiny quills and they got them with their terrible nets. They dragged away everything except the bushy white rabbits who lived quietly, as quietly as they could. They didn't make a sound. They escaped the best they could till the day they came back with their terrible noises and their terrible sound for every thing with white bushy tails that hop.

The little rabbit hid in the high bushes and he saw all that was left being taken away by the terrible things, by the terrible noises, the terrible smells, and then all was quiet in the forest. The little rabbit hopped away to tell others before it was their turn, before it was too late. "Something," he said, "is happening here! There is a man with a gun out there telling you to stop and take care. You better stop children and look around. "Something heavy is coming down."

Chapter 20

Planning the 50ᵗʰ Commemoration of the Warsaw Ghetto Uprising

Ma nishtana halailah hazeh mikol haleilot?
(Why is this day any different from
any other day of the year?)

The call to plan for the 50ᵗʰ Commemoration began in June, 1992 almost immediately after the 49ᵗʰ event. It was a propitious time to be focusing on it. Not since the Nazi period of the 1930s had there been such an alarming rise in the rate of anti-Semitism, racist vandalism against synagogues, cemeteries, and Jewish shops here in the U.S. and abroad.

The concern of the Midwest Jewish Council members was that the next generation needed to be educated to expose anti-Semitism, racism, neo-Nazism, bigotry, prejudice, and fascist oppression.

In the early summer of 1992, Michael Kotzin of the Jewish Community Relations Council of Chicago invited eighteen Jewish community organizations, including MJC and Sheerit Hapleitah to come together in an effort to arrange a unified, all-community 50ᵗʰ Commemoration.

Despite the continued effort and meetings, there appeared insufficient common ground for a unified commemoration.

By the end of October 1992, leaders at MJC were proceeding with their own plans and explained their position in a letter to Michael Kotzin and the Jewish Community Relations Council:

> On July 15, 1992, you called a meeting to plan the 50ᵗʰ Commemoration of the Uprising in the Warsaw Ghetto and pay homage to the six million Jewish Martyrs and millions of others that perished during Hitler's Holocaust. While it would be good if we could have a large citywide memorial, many of our members feel we should be prepared IF a united commemoration does not materialize. We are

anxious to work with you. Unless we hear from you soon, please understand that we will have to plan our own commemoration. We have discussed one unified memorial in the past in 1972 and 1982. Our disagreements no longer center on communism, but on whether issues other than the Holocaust should be discussed. These issues include: Vietnam, anti-Semitism, racism, criticism of Israel and secular Jews.

Apparently such an outreach failed to create the hoped for response. There were other issues as well keeping the community apart, including the long-held resentment felt by many organizations that the Federation had been silent on the commemorations for fifty years.

Thus, by November, the MJC had given up hope for a unified program and invited representatives of Jewish organizations to join them for a brunch and planning session at Loyola Field House.

Although preliminary plans had been discussed at monthly forums, little had actually been done except to make reservations for the Mather High School auditorium. The program committee met in December at Naomi Faigen's apartment in order to take on some critical tasks.

Former Illinois Supreme Court Justice Seymour Simon was asked to be the guest speaker and accepted.

In keeping with the past practice of speakers who were known for their expertise. The Council hastily set up committees to maintain contact with the participants.

Members wrote letters soliciting ads for the program book. Income from these ads had paid for the hall rental, postage, printing, and monthly forums. Monthly forum speakers included outspoken City Hall machine fighter, Alderwoman Helen Schiller who reported on events at the Chicago City Council. Members from the Jewish Serbian Friendship Society, Betsy Lalich and Steve Pinto both discussed the latest developments of the fighting in Yugoslavia.

Philip Prale, a teacher working with the group, "Facing History and Ourselves," discussed anti-Semitism and racism. In

January, Lillian Polus Gerstner, Executive Director of the Holocaust Foundation of Illinois detailed that organization's plans. And finally in March, MJC's own Gerry Revzin discussed the work of the Congress of Secular Jewish Organizations. .

In the meantime, the coordinators wrote a plethora of letters. There were drafts requesting proclamations for the commemoration from Chicago Mayor Richard M. Daley and Illinois Governor Jim Edgar.

Special invitations went out to dignitaries and organizations soliciting sponsorship.Unable to rely completely on volunteers, as had been in the past Rebecca Sive, of the Sive Group was hired to send publicity to newspapers, and radio and TV stations.

A number of organizational sponsors are worthy of note: The American Jewish Committee; the AJCongress; Sholem Asch Reading Circle; Chicago Committee to Defend the Bill of Rights; Chicago Friends of Peace Now; Clergy and Laity Concerned; Congress of Secular Jewish Organizations of North America; Jewish Serbian Friendship Society; National Alliance Against Racist and Political Repression; National Council of Jewish Women; Social Justice Religious Resource Network (SoJuRN); and the Emma Lazarus Jewish Women's Clubs--long-time supporter of MJC. (In 1947 this group was knitting sweaters for orphaned children.) In addition, the event earned sponsorship from the Jewish Council on Urban Affairs, whose Executive Director, Jane Ramsey had been a consistent supporter, and co-chair of many of the annual commemorations and the Jewish Cultural Clubs,

Throughout this history, Zolman Emyanitoff, President of the Jewish Cultural Clubs, played a vital role and deserves a special mention. In 1975, he was the speaker at the commemoration in 1977 he co-chaired the program; in 1979 he became vice-president. Jane Ramsey joined Emyanitoff as co-chair from 1984 through 1988.

Other supporters include the Holocaust Association of Child Survivors and the Association of Children of Holocaust Survivors, the Holocaust Memorial Foundation of Illinois. The Foundation's President, Erna Gans spoke for the group at several meetings.

Milton Herst, Zolman Emyanitoff, George Landman and other board members took on the detail work such as contacting participants for biographies and setting up the order of speakers.

With the time pressure mounting, George Landman was able to pull the program book together with the help of Lester Schlosberg just three weeks before the event.

Many of the 1,000 people who filled the auditorium at Mather High School contributed to the more than 100-page program book, which, in addition to the Memorials to the Six Million Martyrs, contained personal tributes and greetings to the living, especially to grandchildren. It is the grandchildren who are especially precious to Jews a testament to the fact that Hitler failed in his goals.

Chapter 21

The 50th Commemoration
of the Warsaw Ghetto Uprising

1993

The stage was carefully planned. Participants were seated in chairs in a row behind the podium, which was decorated with a poster of the Commander of the Warsaw Ghetto revolt, Mordechai Anielewicz. The photo had been copied from the statue at Kibbutz Yad Mordechai, in Israel.

Two posters dominated the back wall of the stage: In Yiddish and in English: "Never to forget" "Never to forgive."

Tables, on which the candles were placed, had been set on both sides of the podium,. The ushers were reminded to be ready to admit the public at 12:30. The program itself began at 1 p.m. sharp.

Beth Zarefsky, Evanston high School student and Social Action Vice President of the Chicago Federation of Temple Youth, opened the program reading a proclamation from Governor Jim Edgar.

President Milton Herst welcomed the audience, reminding them that the founders of the Midwest Jewish Council had realized anti-Semitism and racism are ingrained in our society and did not end with World War II.

He pointed out to the audience of the current revival of neo-fascism and anti-Semitism cropping up throughout the world. He spoke of Texas where the library administration was banning such books as *Anne Frank* and the *Wizard of Oz.* The Germans had burned books. Herst continued:

> We dare not forget who we are and why we are here. We are people driven by Jewish values to care for the lonely, the weak the poor, the disabled and the dispossessed because we are all God's children. We as Jews have a precious opportunity and the indeed the responsibility to seek harmony and unity among

ourselves. We need to believe in each other and create bridges of understanding to all groups in building a better, more peaceful world.

He then introduced Cantor David Politzer and pianist, Sonia Kass who led the audience in singing the National Anthem and Hatikvah. Rabbi Capers Funnye, Temple Beth Shalom Ethiopian Hebrew Congregation gave the invocation acknowledging "the bravery of our brethren," and at the same time, deploring the "crimes against humanity in, Bosnia-Herzegovina and Liberia where, the struggle against tyranny persists."

Before introducing the speakers, vice president and program chair, Zolman Emyanitoff noted that the previous week had been the Pesach Seder, similar to that of the Warsaw Ghetto fighters. Co-chair Beth Zarefsky described the 1991 resolution at the National Federation of Temple Youth to remember the deaths of the eleven million and to actively engage in public education."The Holocaust," she said, "must be heard by the younger generation. Youth continues the cry, 'never again.'"

The next speaker, "the righteous Gentile," was Dr. F. Burton Nelson, Professor of Theology at North Park College, teacher at the Oxford Center for Hebrew Studies, author of many books and a ten-year participant in the commemorations,

Dr. Nelson reported on the poignant opening of the new Holocaust Museum in Washington, D.C. Six years earlier, he had attended the ceremony of laying the corner-stone. He quoted a disturbing study indicating that the "majority of American high school students and one-third of adults do not know about the Holocaust."

The MJC was proud to honor Mrs. Stanislawa Izraelowicz-Kowalcyk; a woman who was awarded in 1993 the Medal of the Righteous Among the Nations for risking her life to save persecuted Jews in Poland during World War II.

The middle segment of the program was full of songs, poems and memories. Byrne Piven, well-known actor and co-artistic director of the Piven Theater Workshop joined his wife, Joyce Piven, a Northwestern University faculty member, Dr. Bernard Beck, and student Stacey Hirsch in reading selections compiled in 1980 for a counter rally against the Nazis in Skokie. The readings, "A Little Lower Than the Angels," began with graffiti on a concentration camp wall and ended with a call to "choose life."

The most moving story of the event was told by Ida Kersz, survivor and volunteer for the Holocaust Memorial Foundation of Illinois and the Association of Holocaust Child Survivors.

Born in Sosrowiec, Poland, her first memory in 1942, at the age of three and a half, was of being herded with her family into a ghetto.

(The Ghetto became the central location for the Nazis to round up Jews living in a variety of European communities. The Jews were often forced to march for days without food or water, then herded together in the Ghetto, again with little access to food, work or other resources to await deportation to the concentration camps.)

> Ida Kersz told of her mother jumping from a window to her death, after being separated from her three children. Ida was given to a Polish family. The family took her in and she survived. Treated as an illegitimate child, she was kept alive by them but she was taught to fear and hate Jews.

> Her father found her after the war. Eventually she was sent to a Jewish orphanage where she was entered into a re-education program and learned about her Jewish roots. She left Poland in 1957.

The audience was in tears as she said, "I remember this happening to me. I lived it. I am a witness to the Holocaust, and no one can deny it."

Keynote speaker Seymour Simon held the audience in rapt attention as he recounted the story of the resistance:

> The historic occurrence stands as probably the most dramatic siege in history. The Warsaw Ghetto Uprising has become a symbol of resistance that brave men and women and even children can wage against inhumanity, against brutality, against terror, against

evil. For Jews, it marked the beginning of the end of humiliation. It made possible the existence of Israel. History is full of brutalities, but none as monstrous to gypsies and non-Jews as well when they spoke out against the barbarism of the Holocaust. This is not only a Memorial, it is also a tribute to life, *L'Chaim*, to non-Jews and Jew alike, and to the State of Israel.

Together let's say: *"Am Yisrael Chai*, the people of Israel live."

The heavy emotion of the drama, the various songs and the searing tales of the survivors had been lifted by Justice Simon's inspiring speech.

The Candle Lighting Ceremony brought back the pain of remembrance. Twelve candles were lit in preparation for the powerful "Passing on the Legacy" ritual that Holocaust survivors had adopted in Jerusalem during June 1981.

First, George Landman presented a section in Yiddish. A survivor read the following English translation:

Deportations, executions, mass graves, death camps, mute prayers, cries of revolt, desperation, torn scrolls, cities and towns, villages and hamlets, the young, the old, the rich, the poor, women, men and children, Ghetto fighters and partisans, scholars and messianic dreamers, ravaged faces, fists raised. Like clouds of fire, all have vanished.

Then a young person from the next generation approached the stage to read a pledge and light a candle:

We dedicate this pledge to you, to parents who suffered and survived; to our grandparents who vanished in the flames; to our brothers and sisters; to more than one million children so brutally murdered; to all six million whose unyielding spiritual and physical resistance, even in the camps and Ghettos, exemplifies our people's commitment to life.

Then, a parental figure replied:

We take this oath, remember becomes the word, to be handed down from father to son, from mother to daughter, from generation to generation. Remember the murderers, the indifferent world, the victims, the Righteous.

Then, all the participants in the Candle Lighting Ceremony responded in unison:

We take this oath that our legacy endures, that our heart and memories burn and burn and will not be consumed. We will never forget and never forgive.

Robin Cook read from Rabbi Arthur Waskow's *Peace and Disarmament*:

We are the generation that stands between the fires. Behind us the fires of Auschwitz. Before us, the threat of nuclear fires that could make our planet into Auschwitz. We light these candles as a symbol for turning destruction into Light; Light to see each other; Light to see in every human face the spark of God, Light to see our faith into the future. As the prophet Zechariah taught, 'not by might and not by power, but by my spirit,' says the Lord of Hosts."

Cantor David Politzer chanted *El Mole Rachamin*, and for the fiftieth year, the audience was moved from tears to triumph by the message of survival with the collective singing of the Partisan Song.

Chapter 22

Three More Years
of Commemorations

At political rallies or sports competitions, cries often resound from, the crowd: "Two more years" or "Four more years" because the people do not want what has been a good run to end.

There was no outcry for the commemorations but there certainly was such a desire. Those who attended year after year found them an opportunity to renew and to reflect as well as to commemorate and, as a consequence, even though the 50th Commemoration could have been a climactic conclusion they did not let it be. They found the energy and devotion to continue them for "three more years."

***

1994

The 51st Commemoration was held April 17,1994 at Mather High School.

Co-chairs were Milton Herst and Zolman Emyanitoff Proclamations were read by Betsy Lalich, Jewish-Serbian Friendship Society.

Cantor, Hasha Musha, sang the National Anthem and Hatikvah with Sonia Kass as pianist. The invocation was given by Rabbi Paula Feldstein with greetings by Dr.F.Burton Nelson; Irma Grundland, a Holocaust child survivor; State Senators Alice Palmer and Howard Carrol; and Robert Meeropol of The Rosenberg Fund for Children.

Songs were by Hasha Musha. The featured speaker was Heather Booth of the Midwest Academy; who spoke on "Women's Resistance in the Holocaust." George Landman in Yiddish "Passing On the Legacy" of the Candle Lighting Ceremony, The English translation was presented by Robin Cook, Willie Weltman, Erica

107

Gilbert-Levin, Rebecca and Ben Melsky, Mike Simon, Adam Bernstein, Adam Fiddler, Franklin Buono, Dana Becker, Judy Tomkins, Amy Robinson, Malka Mittelman-Seifert.

The candle lighters were: Morris and Samuel Applebaum, Laura Bernstein, Lilo Cohn, Morry Fiddler, Inbal and Yarden Fraiman, Renee Gilbert-Levin, Sam Kersz, Susan Melsky, Eli Oliff, Abby and Sema Reiss, Jim Simon, Sharon Weltman as well as Adele Zaveduk. *El Mole Rachamim* was performed by Cantor Hasha Musha. Sonia Kass was the pianist. And the Partisan Song.

***

1995

The 52nd Commemoration was held April 23, 1995 also at Mather High School. It was co-sponsored by the Spertus Institute and the Midwest Jewish Council. The theme of the program was "From Uprising to Liberation" Dr. Byron L. Sherwin, vice president of the Spertus Institute, was the chairman.

Milton Herst and Zolman Emyanitoff read proclamations.

Joanna Turska, a Polish-Jewish musician, and daughter of a Holocaust survivor gave a musical presentation. Cantor Hasha Musha sang two Jewish songs.

Two clergymen, Father John Pawlikowski and Lutheran minister Reverend Dr. Walter Michel, spoke on "Churches' Efforts at Reconciliation with the Jewish People."

At the Candle Lighting Ceremony, Gerry Revzin read a Yiddish poem with readers of the English translation being: Cara Spitner, Howard Wolke; Laurel Felt, Toby Ehrlich, Nava Cohen and Carol Edelson. Henry Jelen. *El Mole Rachamim* was chanted by Rabbi Yechiel Eckstein.

***

1996

The final Commemoration of the Warsaw Ghetto Uprising—the 53rd—was held April 14, 1996 at Mather High School. It was co-sponsored by the Midwest Jewish Council and the Holocaust Memorial Foundation of Illinois.

The National Anthem and the Hatikvah were sung by Cantor Hasha Musha, acompanied by pianist Sonia Kass. The invocation was given by Rabbi Lawrence Montrose. Proclamations were read by Lisa Derman.

The co-chairs were Zolman Emyanitoff and Erna Gans.

Greetings and remarks were made by Professor William Hill, Loyola University; Dr. Margaret Burroughs, founder of the DuSable Museum of African-American History; Milton Herst; and Lillian Polus Gerstner, director of the Holocaust Museum of Illinois.

The speaker: Chicago University Professor Martha Roth, who spoke on "Writing and Rewriting History; Revisionism as Deception."

The Candle Lighting Ceremony included "Passing on the Legacy." Toby Ehrlich spoke in Yiddish. *El Mole Rachamim* was chanted by Hasha Musha, with accompaniment by Sonia Kass on the piano. The Partisan Song closed the program.

An Afterword

The memorial efforts outlived the life spans of many who had become a part of it. The commemoration of the Holocaust today an expanded event is now a standard part of yearly Jewish activities. American Jews now attend Yom Hashoah (Shoah = memorials) programs in synagogues across the country. There are books, histories, testimonials to be read and television programs depicting stories about the Holocaust to be viewed.

Holocaust memorial foundations have sprung up in a number of cities—with Washington, D.C. housing the largest and most visited center. It was established as part of the Smithsonian complex. The

Candles

late Congressman Sidney R. Yates and his wife, Adeline, worked diligently for the Holocaust Museum to become a reality. Many people who did survive both the Holocaust and specifically the Warsaw Ghetto Uprising have dedicated themselves to educate the younger generations in schools and colleges.

Chapter 23

Illinois HB3 and Education About the Holocaust

(Note: The following chapter is added because the issue is central to both the Midwest Jewish Council and the Holocaust Memorial Foundation of Illinois)

In November 1987, an outbreak of vandalism was directed against Jewish stores and synagogues. It prompted Erna I. Gans, then president of the Holocaust Memorial Foundation of Illinois, to issue a call for action. This was directed to the Chicago Public Schools Board of Education, parochial school leaders and the State of Illinois to encourage them to combat such violence with education in the form of mandatory matter on the Holocaust.

In the months to follow, Mrs. Gans and others HMFI leaders began an investigation of the state of Holocaust education locally and nationwide, compiling data from as many as a dozen states. Armed with this information, they wrote and visited legislators, urging them to validate the need for mandating the teaching of the Holocaust in the form of legislation.

By the spring of 1988, State Representatives Lee Preston, Cal Sutker, Grace Mary Stern, Ellis Levin and Lou Lang had sponsored House Bill 3011.

Erna Gans and educator, Dr. Reading Dallal went to Springfield in the latter part of April 1988 to testify on behalf of the Bill before the Elementary and Secondary Educational Committee of the Illinois House. A vote of 14 in favor and 8 against brought the Bill out of committee to the floor of the House, where the Bill passed by a vote of 80-60, sending it to the State Senate. The Bill failed to pass the Senate's review, however, due primarily to legislators feeling they had insufficient data to make an informed decision.

Undaunted, the Foundation undertook a statewide survey of school administrators and teachers, compiling data regarding existing attempts to teach the Holocaust, on willingness and commitment training and for resource materials to be provided.

111

Within one year, through the direct efforts of the Foundation, the concept of mandating Holocaust education in Illinois, now known as House Bill 3, had resurfaced in the Illinois General Assembly, where it passed both House and Senate.

To insure that former Governor James Thompson signed HB3, Mrs. Gans and the Foundation spearheaded a letter writing and phone campaign, urging the Governor to sign the legislation before the September 17, 1989, deadline. The efforts were successful and Foundation leadership was present to witness the Bill's signing. In 1990, the Illinois School Code Act was drafted by the Holocaust Memorial Foundation of Illinois, requiring that:

> Every public elementary school and high school shall include in its curriculum a unit of instruction studying the events of the Nazi Atrocities of 1933 to 1945 known as the Holocaust. With this, Illinois became the first state in the entire country to mandate the teaching of the Holocaust in all public elementary and high schools. Though some compromises had to be made, the long and arduous process resulted in landmark legislation—that would not have come into being if not for the initiative and involvement of Holocaust Survivors.

Holocaust studies in the schools are an important part of the mission of the Holocaust Memorial Foundation of Illinois, and with common interests, also part of the MJC's concerns.

The Holocaust Studies law became an inconvenience if not a thorn to some in the North Shore suburbs. A band of Winnetka, Illinois, parents decided to try to overturn the Illinois law requiring the teaching of the Holocaust claiming that "the Holocaust is a myth, a Zionist plot to raise money, that there were no gas chambers and no plan to exterminate."

At the 48th Commemoration Revzin showered praise on Charles J. Meyers, an instructor at New Trier High School, who wrote about his experiences. The teacher told of his efforts to bring in a survivor of Thierenstadt concentration camp so that the survivor might share the message of the Holocaust with the children in his class. Meyers wrote:

A humanist Holocaust curriculum emphasizes that people control circumstances, that there is no nebulous inevitability about the events that affect us. I teach the Holocaust to raise awareness of events that affected so many millions and by doing so I instill the determination that those events must never happen again. Otherwise, the victims will die a second death, not by killing and torture, but through ignorance.

The Holocaust is not only about Jews; it is a story for all of us. The lessons we learned from the Holocaust will have no meaning unless we respond to the struggles of freedom loving people throughout the world, to the great concern of saving the environment and wiping out disease and hunger.

We have a responsibility to those who perished in the Warsaw Ghetto. We have inherited from them the mantle of educating people. Jews and non-Jews must be sensitive to the menace of anti-Semitism and racism wherever it may occur.

We pledge to the martyrs who perished in the Holocaust that we shall pass on to each generation the heroism of the Jewish Ghetto fighters, the Jewish Partisan brigades, the images that are vital for the historical memory of the Jewish people and of all humanity.

Wherever the struggle for freedom goes on, in South Africa, Iraq, Kuwait, Eastern Europe, and wherever people seek a homeland and to be free, may the spirit and determination of the Warsaw Ghetto martyrs inspire them in their struggle for ultimate victory."

The names of some of these are included, as best the editors of the book could do so, in the following records kept of the programs.

There were other educators on the same program. Rabbi Daniel Leifer of the Hillel Foundation at the University of Chicago gave the D'var Torah or the speech appropriate to the specific Torah reading of the week.

Educator, activist, and Chicago black community leader, Jacky Grimshaw spoke, as did Dr. F. Burton Nelson of North Park College. Dr.Nelson, always a friend of MJC, read the inscription on the recently published book about the Reverend Diedrich Bonhoffer, a young pastor in the 1930s who dared to speak out. He joined the underground and was imprisoned in 1943 and executed in 1945 for treason against the state. Dr. Nelson's writings were used to honor Bonhoffer; who was installed as a "righteous Gentile" at Yad Vashem.

Dr.Nelson read the dedication on his title page, as he presented his book:

To the Midwest Jewish Council on the 48th Commemoration of the Warsaw Ghetto Uprising, in deep appreciation for the excellent way you keep before us the remembrance of the heroic Uprising of 1943. It is a privilege to join hands with you in the ongoing battle against anti-Semitism, against neo-Nazism, against racism, against bigotry and against prejudice. Shalom.

Programs of the Commemorations of The Warsaw Ghetto Uprising

1944-1993

1stCommemoration May 1, 1944 Orchestra Hall;
Chair: Judge Harry Fisher. Speaker: Rabbi Solomon Goldman.

2nd Commemoration April 18, 1945 in the Hamilton Hotel.
Speaker: Jack Fishbein, editor of *The Sentinel*.

3rdCommemoration April17,1946 at the Albany Park Hebrew
Congregation.Co-Chair: Rabbi Abraham E. Abramowitz,
Albany Park Congregation. Speakers: Rabbi Charles F Shulman,
Glencoe; Samuel Hoffman, attorney; Herman Bush, President; Albert
Brown; chairman of the American Federation of Polish Jews.
El Mole Rachamim and Psalms; Cantor: Louis Shalinsky,
accompanied by Synagogue Choir.
Songs; Miss Llamay Handel, soprano. Poems: Maurice Mason.

4th Commemoration, April 13, 1947 at the Stevens Hotel.
Chair:Judge Harry Fisher. Speakers: Congressman Emanuel Celler;
Sygmund Fbisiak, Polish Consul General; Louis Zara, author.
El Mole Rachamim. Cantor: Moses Rontall.
(Dinner attended by 1,200 persons with many turned away.)

5thCommemoration, April 17, 1948 at the Jewish People's Institute.
Chair: Max Bressler, president, Chicago AJCongress.
Speakers: Josef Winiewicz, Polish Ambassador;
Rabbi Abraham E. Abramowitz, president AFPJ.
Music and *El Mole Rachamim* Cantor: Moses Rontall.
(Ghetto Memorial in Warsaw unveiled April 19, 1948.)

6th Commemoration, May 7,1949 at Orchestra Hall.
Chair: Herman Bush; Music and *El Mole Rachamim*

Cantor: Michal Kusevitsky.
7th Commemoration April 15, 1950 at the Midland Hotel.
Chair: Herman Bush. Speakers: James Waterman Wise,
Council Against Intolerance; Rabbi Abraham Abramowitz;
Judge Harry Fisher; Boris Steinberg; Max Bressler;
Charles Komaiko. Music Cantor: B. Landsman;
Dramatic presentation: Vivian Goldstein.

8th Commemoration, April 29, 1951 at the Sherman House.
Chair: Herman Bush. Yidish Speaker: Rabbi A. Abramowitz.
Speakers: Keith Wheeler, war correspondent for the Sun-Times;
   J.I.Fishbein;Rabbi Samuel Teitelbaum,Northwestern University
Hillel
Boris Steinberg. Candle Lighting Ceremony:
Mrs.Oscar Moskovitz (Ann Hirsch) President of Mizrachi. Women
El Mole Rachamim and *Kaddish:*
Cantor Harold Brindel, Beth-El Temple.Closing with the audience
singing the Partisan Song.

9th Commemoration, April 26, 1952 at the Sherman House.
Chair: Herman Bush. Speakers: S. B. Komaiko,
 Rabbi A. E. Abramowitz; Jack Fishbein.
 Drama: "Megillah of the Ghetto" written by Ben Aronin,
 interpreted by Rosylin Harvey.
Candle Lighting Ceremony: Mrs. Oscar Moskowitz.
 El Mole Rachamim and *Kaddish:* Cantor Harold Brindel. Partisan
Song.

10th Commemoration, April 4, 1953 at the Sherman House.
Chair: Herman Bush. Speakers: Rabbi A. E. Abramowitz;
 Samuel A. Hoffman, Banker. Drama "Megillah of the Ghetto,"
written by Ben Aronin and interpreted by Pearl Harand.
Candle Lighting Ceremony: Mrs. Oscar Moskowitz.
El Mole Rachamim and *Kaddish:* Cantor Moses J. Silverman,
 Ashe Emet.Congregation. Partisan Song.

11th Commemoration, April 10, 1954 at the Palmer House.
Chair: Herman Bush. Invocation: Rabbi Alvin Kleinerman,
Cong. B'nai Sholom. Speakers: Rabbi A.E.Abramowitz;
Samuel A. Hoffman.Historic Drama: Howard DaSilva and Jacob
Ben-Ami. Candle Lighting Ceremony: Ann Laskin.
El Mole Rachamim and *Kaddish:* Cantor Moses J. Silverman.
Partisan Song.

12th Commemoration, April 17, 1955 at the Palmer House.
Chair: Herman Bush. Invocation: Rabbi Aaron Rine
Cong. BethYitzchok. Speakers: Rabbi A.E.Abramowitz; Esther
Fire.
Drama: "These We Remember." written by Ben Aronin.
Cantor: Moses J. Silverman, Elaine Skorodin, violin.
Candle Lighting Ceremony, Ann Laskin. *El Mole Rachamim* and
Kaddish: Rabbi S. Burr Yampol. Partisan Song.

13th Commemoration April 15, 1956 at the Palmer House Hotel.
Chair: Herman Bush. Invocation Rabbi S. Burr Yampol; Phil Brail,
Harry Fridin, S. B. Komaiko. Speakers: Rabbi A. E. Abramowitz,
Ann Laskin, Boris Steinberg. Drama: "The Trial of Peter Schultz"
by Ben Aronin with Everett Clarke. Cantor: Moses J. Silverman;
Erwin Jospe, Oratorio choir.
Candle Lighting Ceremony: Ann Laskin. *El Mole Rachamim* and
Kaddish: Rabbi Shraga Abarbanel. Partisan Song.

14th Commemoration, April 7, 1957 at the Palmer House.
Chair: Herman Bush.
Speakers: Ben Zion Goldberg, historian and columnist;
Rabbi A.E.Abramowitz.Drama "Mourning To Morning," Everett
Clarke
written by Ben Aronin.
Candle Lighting Ceremony;Ann Laskin, Johanna Starkopf.
El Mole Rachamim and *Kaddish:*
Cantor Harold Brindel. Partisan Song.

15th Commemoration, April 6, 1958 at the Sherman House.
Chair: Herman Bush and Philip Brail.Invocation: Rabbi Aaron M.
Rine, Cong. Beth Yitzchok. Speakers: Rabbi S.Burr Yampol;
Rabbi A.E.Abramowitz (from Israel).
Drama: "The Great Hour" by Ben Aronin, with Studs Terkel,
Everett Clarke.
Cantor Pavel Slavensky, Sulie and Pearl Harrand.
Candle Lighting Ceremony: Ann Laskin, Ciporah Fox Katz
Rabbi Ephraim Prombaum, Donald Sokol, Phylis Polakow.
El Mole Rachamim and *Kaddish*: Cantor Pavel Slavensky, Temple
Sholom. Partisan Song.

16th Commemoration, April 6, 1959 at the Palmer House.
Chair: Herman Bush. Invocation, Rabbi S. Burr Yampol.
Speakers: Rabbi Carl Richter, Sinai Temple, Michigan City;
Rabbi A. E. Abramowitz. Drama; "We Hear Their Voices" by Ben
Aronin. Cantor: Moses Silverman.Paul Barnes, Halevi Choral
Society accompanied by Sonia Gamburg Kass, directed by Hyman
Resnick.
Candle Lighting Ceremony: Ann Laskin.
Partisan Song.

17th Commemoration, April 7, 1960 at the Palmer House Hotel
Co-Chair: Herman Bush, S.L.Talmy. Invocation: Rabbi Aaron M.
Rine. Speakers: Ohio Senator Stephen M. Young; businessman
Mandel Terman; Honorable Stefan Rogozinski, Poland's Consul
General for Chicago. Drama; "And Still They Marched" by Ben
Aronin; Everett Clarke;
Morris Carnowsky.
Cantor Moses Silverman, Erwin Jospe and Theatre Players.
Candle Lighting Ceremony: Ann Laskin. *El Mole Rachamim* and
Kaddish: Rabbi S. Burr Yampol. Partisan Song.

18th Commemoration, April 9, 1961 at the Palmer House Hotel.
Chair: Herman Bush, S.L. Talmy. Invocation: Rabbi Aaron M. Rine.
Candle Lighting Ceremony: Ann Laskin,

Speakers: Senator Wayne Morse, Oregon; Rabbi A. E. Abramowitz;
Gerry Revzin. Drama: "Eichman's Accomplices" by Ben Aronin, starring Howard DaSilva. Cantor Moses Silverman, Everett Clarke, Erwin Jospe.
El Mole Rachamim and *Kaddish:* Rabbi S. Burr Yampol. Partisan Song.

19th Commemoration, April 15, 1962 at McCormick Place.
National Anthem and *Hatikvah*, Edward Firestone.
Invocation:Rabbi Malcolm Cohen.Co-Chair: Herman Bush, S.L.Talmy.
Speakers: Hon. Theodore R. Mckedlin, Governor of Maryland,
Judge Abraham Lincoln Marovitz. Drama:"Epic of the Warsaw Ghetto"
by Ben Aronin and "Babi Yar" by Eugene Yevtushenko,
starring Everett Clarke. Cantor Moses Silverman.
Candle Lighting Ceremony: Mrs. Margaret Kolb, Yiddish. Gerry Revzin. Resolutions: Phil Brail, Rabbi S. Burr Yampol
Drama: Cantor Moses Silverman, Dee Clark, Gil Podolner,
Barbara Dombre, John Tibbs, Jim Fesler, Peter Irmiter. Partisan Song.

20th Commemoratio, April 7, 1963 at the Sherman House.
Co-Chair: Herman Bush, Samual L.Talmy.Invocation:
Rabbi Malcolm Cohen. Candle Lighting Ceremony: Mrs. Issac Kolb,
Mrs. Martin Katz; survivors.
Speakers:Ohio Senator Stephen M.Young;Rabbi A. E. Abramowitz;
Sidney Lens, AFL-CIO; Rabbi S. Burr Yampol. Drama: "Guilty"
by Ben Aronin, starring Everett Clarke, Cantor Moses Silverman, Erwin Jospe. Resolutions: Phil Brail. Partisan Song.

21st Commemoration, April 9, 1964 at the Conrad Hilton Hotel Co-Chair:Herman Bush, Samuel Talmy. Invocation: Rabbi Malcolm Cohen. Yiddish: Gerry Revzin. Candle Lighting Ceremony: Luther Adler. Cantor Moshe Kusevitsky. Drama "Warsaw Ghetto Uprising" with Howard DaSilva, Speakers: Hon. Edward Drozniak, Polish Ambassador; Herman Shumlin, producer and director of "The Deputy." Resolutions: Phil Brail. Partisan Song.

22nd Commemoration, April 11, 1965 at the Conrad Hilton hotel. National Anthem and *Hatikvah*: Cantor Harold Brindell. Invocation: Rabbbi Malcolm Cohen. Singer Hanna Ahron Co-Chairs: Herman Bush and Ann Laskin Hirsch; Yiddish, Gerry Revzin;. Drama: Nehemiah Persoff. Candle Lighting Ceremony: six survivors. Cantor: Harold Brindell. Speakers: Senator Wayne Morse, Oregon; Reverend Paul E. Turner, Coordinator Mayor's Citizen Committee. Rabbi S. Burr Yampol. Resolutions: Phil Brail. Partisan Song

23rd Commemoration, April 17, 1966 at the Conrad Hilton Hotel National Anthem: *Hatikvah*. Cantor: Harold Brindell. Invocation; Rabbi Arnold Jacob Wolf.Co-Chair: Herman Bush, and Ann Hirsch. Candle Lighting Ceremony; six survivors. Songs: Sidor Belarsky. Drama; Everett Clarke, Yiddish. Speaker:Gerry Revzin; Reverend James Bevel, West Side Christian Parish; Oregon Senator Wayne Morse.Resolutions: Phil Brail. Partisan Song.

24th Commemoration, April 9, 1967 at the Conrad Hilton Hotel. National Anthem and *Hatikvah*, Phil Levinson. Speaker: Rabbi Abraham L.Feinberg, Toronto. Yiddish, Gerry Revzin Invocation: Rabbi S. Burr Yampol. Co-chair: Herman Bush; Ann Hirsch and Rabbi Emeritus A .E. Abramowitz.. Candle Lighting Ceremony: six survivors. *El Mole Rachamim* and Songs: Sidor Belarsky, accompanied by Zina Aleskow. Drama: Baruch Lumet, actor, accompanied by Sonia Kass. Resolutions Phil Brail. Partisan Song.

25th Commemoration, April 21, 1968 at the Palmer House.
National Anthem and *Hatikvah*. Cantor: Pavel Slavensky.
Invocation: Rabbi Menahim M. Goodman; Gerry Revzin, Yiddish.
Chair Ann Hirsch. Candle Lighting Ceremony: six survivors.
El Mole Rachamim and songs, Cantor Louis Danto accompanied
by Sonia Kass. Speakers: Senator Ernest Gruening, Alaska.
Resolutions: Phil Brail. Partisan Song.

26th Commemoration, April 20, 1969 at the Sherman House.
National Anthem and *Hatikvah*: Cantor Pavel Slavensky.
Invocation: Rabbi Menahim M. Goodman. Chair: Ann Hirsch.
Drama "A Scene from the Wall" by Adult Theatre of Henry Hart,
Jewish Community Center directed by Eddie Goldberg.
Speaker: Congressman Abner J. Mikva.
Resolutions: Phil Brail. Candle Lighting Ceremony.
El Mole Rachamim: Cantor Pavel Slavensky. Partisan Song.

27th Commemoration April 12, 1970 at the Sheridan Plaza Hotel.
National Anthem and *Hatikvah*: Cantor Norton H. Siegal.
Invocation: Rabbi Menahim M. Goodman.
Co-chairs: Elias Picheny, Ann Hirsch. Speaker: Abe Feinglass,
vice president, AMC& BW Union.
Drama Youth of South Side School of Jewish Studies. Partisan
Song.

28th Commemoration, April 25, 1971 at Northeastern Illinois
State College. National Anthem and *Hatikvah*: Cantor Maurice
Goldberg.
Invocation: Rabbi Menahim M.Goodman.
Co-chair: Robert Herbin and Ann Hirsch. Charlotte Rosen,
Yiddish.
Drama: Chicago Jewish Peoples Choral Society, led by Julius
Schwarztein, Rose Fogelman Sang and led the Youth Ensemble.
Speaker: State Representitive. Robert E. Mann, past president, B'nai
B'rith. Partisan Song.

29th Commemoration, April 16, 1972 at the LaSalle Hotel.
National Anthem, *Hatikvah*: Cantor Philip Marantz.
Invocation: Rabbi Menahim M. Goodman. Yiddish, Joseph Rosen
Co-chair: Ann Hirsch and Robert Herbin.. Speaker: Joseph M.
Jacobs, labor lawyer. Drama: Chicago Jewish People's Choral
Society, directed
by Jerry Litan with Ann Hyman.Bernard Warman and Rose
Fogelman
led the Youth Ensemble. Partisan Song.

30th Commemoration, April 8, 1973 at Mather High School
Auditorium. National Anthem and *Hatikvah*: Cantor Eliyahu
Schleifer. Invocation: Rabbi Menahim M. Goodman.
Co-chair: Ann Hirsch, Robert Herbin; Joseph Rosen, Yiddish.
Drama: "Babi Yar" narrated by Sara Lieberman.
Speaker: Abe Feinglass, vice president AMC&BW Union.
Soloists; Rose Fogelman, Edward Rodrigues, Wayne Staley,
Jewish Peoples Choral Society, directed by Jerry Litan.
Ann Hyman, pianist. Candle Lighting Ceremony: Women from the
chorus. *El Mole Rachamim* by Cantor Eliyahu Schleifer. Partisan
Song.

31st Commemoration, April 31, 1974 at Mather High School.
National Anthem and *Hatikvah*: Cantor Eliyahu Schleifer.
Invocation: Rabbi Menahim M. Goodman.Chair Ann Hirsch
Speaker: Zolman Emyanitoff, president, Jewish Cultural Clubs of
Chicago. Candle Lighting Ceremony. Musical: Rose Fogelman,
Soprano.
Partisan Song.

32nd Commemoration, April 20, 1975 at Mather High School.
National Anthem and *Hatikvah*: Cantor Eliyahu Schleifer.
Invocation: Rabbi Menahim M. Goodman.
Co-chair: Zolman Emyanitoff and Ann Hirsch. Joseph Rosen
Yiddish. Speakers: Charles A. Hayes, vice president, AMC and
BW, Illinois State AFL-CIO and vice president, National Coalition

of Black Trade Unionists. Irving Steinberg, civil rights attorney.
Musical: "Faith In Our People."
Rose Fogelman, soprano; Esther Levinson, piano. Candle Lighting
Ceremony, *El Mole Rachamim*, Cantor Eliyahu Schleifer. Partisan
Song.

33rd Commemoration, April 11, 1976 at Mather High School.
National Anthem and *Hatikvah*: Cantor Pavel Slavensky.
Invocation: Rabbi Menahim M. Goodman. Joseph Rosen, Yiddish
Co-chair: Ann Hirsch, Jack Altman..Speaker: Irving Steinberg, civil
rights attorney. Candle Lighting Ceremony, *El Mole Rachamim*,
Cantor Pavel Slavensky. Drama: "The Diary of Anne Frank,"
Jewish Community Center of Milwaukee Players.
Partisan Song.

34th Commemoration, April 17, 1977 at Mather High School.
National Anthem and *Hatikvah*, Cantor Eliyahu Schleifer.
Invocation: Rabbi Menahim M. Goodman.
Co-Chair: Zolman Emyanitoff and Ann Hirsch. Jack Altman, Yiddish.
Speaker: Professor Irwin Weil; Chairman, Slavic Department,
Nothwestern University. Poems: Jeffrey Sanders, student.
Resolutions: Dorothy Scheinberg, Zolman Emyanitoff.
Candle Lighting Ceremony: Ann Hirsch, Muriel Berson,
Francis Brickman, Sara Horwitz, Ann Leavitt, Dorothy Scheinberg,
Marion Talmy. *El Mole Rachamim*, Cantor Pavel Slavensky. Partisan
Song

35th Commemoration, April 16, 1978 at Mather High School.
National Anthem and *Hatikvah*: Cantor Pavel Slavensky.
Invocation:Rabbi Menahim M. Goodman. Jack Altman, Yiddish
Co-chair: Ann Hirsch and Zolman Emyanitoff.. Speaker: Irving
Steinberg, civil rights attorney. Drama: Paul Barnes and Dorothy
Jordon.
Candle Lighting Ceremony. Vocalist: Pavel Slavensky,
 accompanied by pianist Sonia Kass. Partisan Song.

36th Commemoration, April 22, 1979 at Mather HighSchool.
National Anthem and *Hatikvah*; Cantor Pavel Slavensky
Invocation:Rabbi Menahim M.Goodman. Joseph Rosen Yiddish.
Co-chair: Ann Hirsch and Zolman Emyanitoff
Music: Joan Bowman, flutist. Sonia Kass, pianist.
Speaker: Abe Feinglass, vice-president AMC&BW Union.
Candle Lighting Ceremony.*El Mole Rachamin,*
Cantor Pavel Slavensky. Partisan Song.

37th Commemoration, April 27, 1980 at Mather High School.
National Anthem and *Hatikvah*, Cantor Pavel Slavensky.
Invocation: Rabbi Menahim M. Goodman. Jack Altman, Yiddish
Co-chair: Ann Hirsch Zolman Emyanitoff,.
"Poem of the Ghetto," Gil Parker. Candle Lighting Ceremony.
Speaker: Charles Nicodemus reporter with the Chicago Sun-Times.
El Mole Rachamim, Cantor Pavel Slavensky. Partisan Song.

38th Commemoration, April 5, 1981 at North Park College.
National Anthem and *Hatikvah*: Cantor Pavel Slavensky.
Invocation: Rabbi Manahim M. Goodman.
Co-chair: Ann Hirsch and Milton Herst. Harry Ferber, Yiddish.
"Instant Of Auschwitz," slides by Alan Jacobs.
Drama by Byrne Piven Theatre Workshop.
Speakers: Esther Fink, Association of Children of Survivors;
Irving G. Steinberg, civil rights attorney. Music: Ruth Habas.
Candle Lighting Ceremony: Frances Brickman, Millie Fellin,
Erna Gans, Sarah Horwitz, Donna Manfield, Jerry Shane,
Debbie Sufrin, Mark Weinberg and Sheldon Rosenbaum.
David Zverow, recorder:*El Mole Rachamim*,
Cantor Pavel Slavensky. Partisan Song.

39th Commemoration, April 25, 1982 at North Park College,
National Anthem and *Hatikvah*: Cantor Pavel Slavensky.
Invocation: Rabbi Jack Frank. Speaker Congressman Harold
Washington
Co-chair: Ann Hirsch, Helene Hoffman and Milton Herst.

124

Candle Lighting Ceremony: George Landman, Yiddish; Lydia Cindy Reich,
Jacob, Sylvia, Morris Applebaum, Bluma and Michael Zolno,
Gittel, Stephen Hunt. Jean, Sheila Beller, Sandor Kirsche. Lynn Shapiro.
El Mole Rachamim; Cantor: Pavel Slavensky, Sonia Kass at piano;
David Zverow, recorder; Laurie Sucher, solist.
Presentation of Am Chai's "Resistance In Bialystock Ghetto"
by Bill Dolnick, Harvey Feldman, Les Friedman, Lynn Kerman,
Kate Kinser, Marsha Perman and Joel Shaffer. Partisan Song
.

40th Commemoration, April 17, 1983 at Mather High School.
National Anthem and *Hatikvah*: Laurie Sucher;
Peter Scheiner, pianist. Invocation; Rabbi Ira Sud.
"Fighters Call To Arms," Muriel Berson,
Co-Chair: Marla Baker and Milton Herst. Opening Remarks: Ann Hirsch. Speakers: Avri Fischer, head of Mapam and Kibbutz, Artzi Federation of Kibbutzim. Adar Rossman, Yiddish, Drama and Songs: "Bashert," Kate Kinser, Laurie Sucher and Marlene Stern.
 Donna Mandel, dance. Candle Lighting Ceremony:Passing on the Legacy
Barbara and Marvin Steiner, Bela, Jack Korn, Naomi Faigen,
Dora Gold Schwartzstein, Joel Jacobson,Tola Pinkus, Miriam Schiller, Bluma and Michael Zolno, David Maureen Figman.
Reading the "Passing on the Legacy," Erna Gans, Zolman Emyanitoff,
El Mole Rachamim; Rabbi Ira Sud, David Zverow, recorder;
 Laurie Sucher, soloist. Partisan Song

41st Commemoration, April 8, 1984 at North Park College.
National Anthem and *Hatikvah*: Cantor Pavel Slavensky.
Invocation: Rabbi Herman Schaalman.
Welcome: Reverend Dr. F. Burton Nelson.
Co-chair: Zolman Emyanitoff and Jane Ramsey.
Speaker: Charles R. Allen Jr., author and lecturer on Nazi war criminals living in the U.S. Second Generation: Toby Ehrlich, Henry Jelen and Miriam Schiller read a Yiddish poem, "Jewish Child."

Candle Lighting Ceremony: George Landman in Yiddish; Zolman Emyanitoff in English. "Passing On the Legacy," Mildred Fellin, Erna Gans, Bela Korn,
Lisa Silbert, Barbara Steiner, Mark Weinberg, Allen Zendel.
El Mole Rachamim, Cantor: Pavel Slavensky; Sonia Kass, Pianist, Gerry Revzin spoke in Yiddish.Drama, "They Fought Back" by Uri Suhl; presented by Florence G. Heller Community Center Ensemble directed by Linda Sherman. Partisan Song.

42nd Commemoration, April 21, 1985 at North Park College
National Anthem and *Hatikvah*, Hasha Musha,
Invocation Rabbi Frederick Wenger.Welcome: Dr.Frederick Holmgren.
Co-Chair: Zolman Emyanitoff and Jane Ramsey.
Speaker: Erwin "Bud" Salk, history teacher at Columbia College; Robert Skeist, Chicago Friends of Peace Now.
Second Generation, Toby Ehrlich, Henry Jelen, Miriam Schiller read a Yiddish poem, "A Lonely Child." Candle Lighting Ceremony.
"Passing On The Legacy," George Landman in Yiddish;
Zolman Emyanitoff and Jane Ramsey in English.
Felice Brenner, Toby Ehrlich, Henry Jelen, Tola Pinkus,
Miriam and Rivka Schiller, Malka Seifert, Barbara Steiner
Allen Zendel lit candles. Kate Kinser spoke in Yiddish
Drama: "A Little Lower Than the Angels" by Byrne and Joyce Piven.
El Mole Rachamim, chanted by Hasha Musha; Sonia Kass, pianist. Partisan Song

43rdCommemoration, April 13, 1986 at North Park College.
National Anthem and *Hatikvah*, Cantor Shlomo Shuster;
Sheldon Rosenbaum, pianist. Invocation: Rabbi Robert J. Marx.
Co-Chair: Zolman Emyanitofff and Gerry Revzin.
Greetings and remarks: Mayor Harold Washington.Dr. F. Burton Nelson. Music; Joan Bowman, flutist; Sonia Kass, pianist. Dramatic presentation: Dina Helpern; Sheldon Rosenbaum, pianist. Candle Lighting Ceremony, "Passing On the Legacy:" George Landman, Yiddish, Zolman Emyanitoff and Toby Ehrlich, in English, Karla

and Otto Grenton, Helene Hoffman, Henry Jellen, Bela Korn, Rochelle Philips, Frieda Reider, Miriam Schiller, Barbara Steiner. Muriel Steiner, Mark Weinberg, Joseph Weisner.
El Mole Rachamim, Cantor Shlomo Shuster; Sheldon Rosenbaum, pianist. Partisan Song

44th Commemoration April 26, 1987 at North Park College,
National Anthem and *Hatikvah*, Cantor David Politzer; Sonia Kass, pianist. Invocation: Rabbi Norman, J. Lewison
Co-chair: Milton Herst, Zolman Emyanitoff and Jane Ramsey.
Greeting and remarks: Mayor Harold Washington .
Dr. F. Burton Nelson, professor at North Park College.
Reverend Hycel Berman Taylor, 2nd Baptist Church Evanston.
Candle Lighting Ceremony. "Passing On the Legacy"
George Landman, Yiddish; Robin Cook, Toby Ehrlich,Helene Hoffman, Miriam Nuedel, Miriam Schiller,Robert Skeist, Elliot Zashin in English David and Ilene Figman, Karla and Otto Grenton, Henry and Dov Jellen,
Renny Kurshenbaum, Judy and Al Lachman, Henry Rosen.
Barbara and Muriel Steiner. *El Mole Rachamim.*CantorDavid Politzer; Sonia Kass, pianist; Roberta Guastafeste, cellist.
Drama:Byrne Piven Workshop. Speaker: Ruth M. Rothstein, chief executive, Mount Sinai and Schwab Medical Center.
Partisan Song

45th Commemoration, April 17, 1988 at Mather High School.
National Anthem and *Hatikvah*, Cantor David Politzer; Sonia Kass, pianist. Invocation: Rabbi Ernest M. Lorge. . Gerry Revzin, Yiddish
Co-chair: Zolman Emyanitoff, Jane Ramsey and Heather Booth.
Greetings: Milton Herst president of the MJC;
Dr. F. Burton Nelson .Dr. Kenneth Smith, Chicago Theological Seminary.
Speaker:Leon M. Despres, labor lawyer, former alderman, educator
Candle Lighting Ceremony. "Passing On the Legacy" George Landman, Yiddish; Robin Cook, Gerald Davidson, Toby Ehrlich, Michael Gaster, Helen Hoffman, Nova Horwitz, Henry Jelen,

Miriam Nuedel. Henry Rosen, Stan Rosen, Miriam Schiller, Robert Skeist, Elliot Zashin in English. Karla Grenton, Werner Lewy, David Figman, Joe and Gita Neumann, Margie Oppenheimer Malka Mittelman Seifert, Ruth Hedvat Shorr, Carla Monica Seifert, Barbara Steiner, lit Candles. Drama, "And The Earth Rebelled" by Yuri Suhl; read by Jerry Jarrett. Partisan Song

46th Commemoration, April 16, 1989 at Mather High School.
National Anthem and *Hatikvah*, Cantor Pavel Slavensky;
Sonia Kass, pianist. Invocation: Rabbi Joseph Allen Edelheight;
Co-chair: Zolman Emyanitoff and Heather Booth
Greetings: Dr. F. Burton Nelson; Reverend Nathaniel Jarrett,
Church Federation of Chicago. Proclamation: Mayor Eugene Sawyer. Speaker: Sondra Gair, broadcast journalist, WBEZ.
Candle Lighting Ceremony: "Passing On the Legacy,"
George Landman; Yiddish, Rachel Abramson, Robin Cook, Toby Ehrlich, Michael Gaster, Miriam Nuedel, Stan Rosen, Malka Mittelman-Seifert, Peggy Shapiro, Ruth Hedvat Shorr, Stuart Starr, Laurie Sucher,
Elliot Zashin, English. Candle lighters: Nava Cohen, Sara Cohn, Yochanan Dreazen, Crystal Henle, Henry Jelen, Lesley Beth Kiselevitz, Renny Kurshenbaum, Eva Rothchild, Carla Monica Seifert, Ari Shapiro.
El Mole Rachamim, Cantor David Politzer; Sonia Kass, pianist.
Partisan Song.

47th Commemoration, April 29, 1990 at Mather High School.
National Anthem and *Hatikvah*; Laurie Sucher, soloist.
Invocation: Rabbi Paul Golomb. Greetings: Dr. F Burton Nelson
Co-chair: Zolman Emyanitoff Sylvia Markowitz Neil
Professor.Timuel Black, concentration camp Liberator. Kate Harris New Jewish Agenda. Candle Lighting Ceremony "Passing On the Legacy" George Landman in Yiddish. Nava Cohen, Robin Cook, Toby Ehrlich, Michael Gaster, Marilyn Grossman, Henry Jelen, Carla Monica Seifert, Malka Mittelman-Seifert, Peggy Shapiro, Laurie Sucher, Andrew White, in English. Candles lighters; Victoria Alkhovsky, Nina Dudnick, Milly Fellin, Nathan Goldfarb, Ruth

Gordon, Dov Jelen. *El Mole Rachamim* chanted by Laurie Sucher. Speaker: Dr. Quentin Young, health and medicine policy group. Drama "Facing History and Ourselves" directed by Chuck Meyers with Phil Brail, Elizabeth Castillo, Vincent Willis, Tara Purohit. Partisan Song.

48th Commemoration, April 14, 1991 at Mather HighSchool.
National Anthem, *Hatikvah*; Cantor: David Politzer. Sonia Kass, pianist. Invocation: Rabbi Daniel Leifer, Hillel of Chicago University.
Chair: Zolmnn Emyanitoff Greetings:
Elliot Zashin, Hillel University of Illinois Chicago. Jacky Grimshaw, educator. Panel: "Impact of the Holocaust on the Jews of Tomorrow;" Rabbi Philip Lefkowitz "Diaspora Jews and Their Relationship with Israel" Rabbi Robert Marx, "Causes and Effects of Anti-Semitism and Racism." Gerry Revzin, "Teaching the Lessons of the Holocaust." Songs Niles Township Jewish Congregation. Junior Choir, conducted by Ms.Cyd Baron. Candle Lighting Ceremony;"Passing On the Legacy"George Landman Yiddish, Rose Blumstein, Nava Cohen, Sara Cohen, Robin Cook,
Toby Ehrlich, Marilyn Grossman,Henry Jelen, Brenda Moss, Stuart Starr, Malka Mittleman-Seifert, Laurie Sucher, Sally Wagner in English.
Candle lighters: Lilly Blayer, Sandi Gaffen, Molly Goldberg, Peter Levin, Mark Weinberg, Karen Cohen, Yochi Dreazen, Anna Tunik, Ann and Michael Livschitz, Rachel Feldheim, Rivka Shiller.*El Mole Rachamim*, Cantor David Politzer; Sonia Kass, pianist.Partisan Song.

49th Commemoration, April 12, 1992 at Mather High School.
National Anthem and *Hatikvah*, Cantor David Politzer; Sonia Kass, pianist. Invocation: Rabbi Yechiel Eckstein. Greetings: Dr. F. Burton Nelson
Welcome and Co-chair: Milton Herst and Zolman Emyanitoff.
Danny Davis, Ph.D., Cook County Commissioner. Drama: Marylin Price, storyteller and puppeteer. Songs: Jewish Reconstructionist Congregation Choir, conducted by Daniel Wallenberg. Speaker:

Lawrence S. Bloom; alderman, introduced by Jane Ramsey. Candle Lighting Ceremony: "Passing On the Legacy" George Landman in Yiddish. Martha Churchill, Robin Cook, Agi DeCanniere, Keren Fraiman, Fritzie Fritzshall,
Oto Grenton, Ida Kersz, Heddy Newman, Shirley Novak, Kari Richmond, Malka Mittelman-Seifert, Leon Stein, in English. Candle lighters:
Jeremy A. and Joshua E. Abraham, Sima Blue, Toby Ehrlich, Leana Ehrlich Jelen, Inbal Fraiman, Susan Katz, Eli Oliff, Abigail Reiss, Adam Richmond, Lisa Silbert, Mark Weinberg, Hanna Weiss, Lillian Zelkowitz. *El Mole Rachamim*, Cantor David Politzer, Sonia Kass, pianist. Partisan Song.

50th Commemoration, April 25, 1993 at Mather High School. Proclamations and welcome: Beth Zerefsky, Chicago Federation of Temple Youth.Program Co-chair: Milton Herst, president, MJC; Zolman Emyanitoff, vice-president. National Anthem and *Hatikvah*, Cantor David Politze; Sonia Kass, pianist. Invocation: Rabbi Capers Funnye, Temple Beth Sholom, Ethiopian Hebrew Congregation. Greetings: Dr. F. Burton Nelson, Professor, North Park College; Ida Kersz, Holocaust child survivor.Songs: Hasha Musha. Drama: Piven Theatre Workshop.
Speaker: Justice Seymour Simon, former Justice of the Illinois Supreme Court. Candle Lighting Ceremony: "Passing On the Legacy," George Landman in Yiddish; Martha Churchill, Nava Cohen, Robin Cook, Karen Fraiman. Irma Grundland, Gittel Hunt, Henry Jelen, Susan Klein, Chaim Levendel, Kari Richmond, Malka Mittelman-Seifert, Adel Zavedu, in English. Candle lighters: Debbie Cohen, Toby Ehrlich, Liana Ehrlich Jelen, Ben Freed, Dr. Felix and Lucy Horn, Betsy Lalich, Steve Pinto, Nechama Schiller, Karen VanAusdal, Josh Weinberg, Mark Weinberg, Lissa Weiss.Ushers: Alex Fishkin, Vadim Fridman, Alex Galperin,
Kirrill Gorokozaky, Julia Kaplunov, Marina Levin.
Judy Hoffman, coordinator. *El Mole Rachamim*, Cantor: David Politzer;
Sonia Kass, pianist. Partisan Song

51st Commemoration, April 17, 1994 at Mather High School. National Anthem, *Hatikvah* and Invocation: Rabbi Paula Feldstein. Greetings: Dr. F. Burton Nelson: Irma Grundland, Holocaust child survivor; State Senators Alice Palmer, and Howard Carrol; and Robert Meeropol, Rosenberg Fund for Children. Songs; Hasha Musha. Milton Herst,
Chair:Zolman Emyanitoff. Speaker: Heather Booth, Midwest Academy, "Women's Resistance in the Holocaust." Candle Lighting Ceremony: "Passing on the Legacy;" George Landman, Yiddish. English Translation: Robin Cook. Willie Weltman, Erica Gilbert-Levin, Rebecca and Ben Melsky, Mike Simon, Adam Bernstein, Adam Fiddler, Franklin Buono, Dana Becker, Judy Tomkins, Amy Robinson, Malka Mittelman-Seifert.
Candle lighters: Morris and Samuel Applebaum, Laura Bernstein, Lilo Cohn, Morry Fiddler, Inbal and Yarden Fraiman, Renee Gilbert-Levin, Sam Kersz, Susan Melsky, Eli Oliff, Abby and Sema Reiss, Jim Simon, Sharon Weltman, Adele Zaveduk. Procalmations: Betsy Lalich,
Jewish-Serbian Friendship Society. *El Mole Rachamim,* Cantor Hasha Musha; Sonia Kass, pianist. Partisan Song

52nd Commemoration April 23, 1995 at Mather High School. Spertus Institute and the Midwest Jewish Council.
"From Uprising to Liberation," Dr. Byron L.Sherwin.
Proclamations: Milton Herst and Zolman Emyanitoff.
Joanna Turska, Polish-Jewish musician and daughter of survivor.
Cantor: Hasha Musha. Church efforts at Reconciliation with the Jewish People: Father John Pawlikowski, Catholic; and
Reverend Dr. Walter Michel, Lutheran. Candle Lighting Ceremony:
Gerry Revzin (read Yiddish poem). English readers: Cara Spitner, Howard Wolke, Laurel Felt, Toby Ehrlich, Nava Cohen, Carol Edelson Henry Jelen. *El Mole Rachamim,* Rabbi Yechiel Eckstein. Partisan Song.

53rd Commemoration, April 14, 1996 at Mather High School. Midwest Jewish Council and Holocaust Memorial Foundation of Illinois. National Anthem and *Hatikvah*, Cantor Hasha Musha; Sonia Kass, pianist. Invocation: Rabbi Lawrence Montrose.

Proclamation: Lisa Derman Co-chairs: Zolman Emyanitoff and Erna Gans. Greetings: Professor. William Hill, Loyola University;

Dr. Margaret Burroughs, founder of DuSable Museum of African-American History; Milton Herst; Lillian Polus Gerstner, director Holocaust Museum of Illinois. Speaker: Professor Martha Roth, Chicago University, "Writing and Rewriting History; Revisionism as Deception."

Candle Lighting Ceremony, "Passing On the Legacy," Toby Ehrlich in Yiddish. *El Mole Rachamim*, chanted by Hasha Musha; Sonia Kass, pianist. Partisan Song

Printed in the United States
20418LVS00005B/103-222